This book is a wonderful e speaks afresh in every genera eye and a kind pastor's 2 Timothy showing us the true roots for resilience in pastoral ministry. This is an exc resource for pastors to keep on keeping on.

ROBIN WEEKES
Minister, Emmanuel Church Wimbledon

For pastors under pressure, John Benton brings help from 2 Timothy so that we can not only survive but grow and flourish in ministry. John speaks from his own experience as a pastor, and his current ministry of supporting others who serve Christ's church. There is much wisdom here not just for pastors but all who seek to serve the Lord.

BILL JAMES
Principal, London Seminary

As one who grew up in the church John pastored for over 30 years, I saw, first-hand, his personal resilience in ministry and the fruit his resilient ministry produced. I am so grateful then, as one in the early days of ministry, that John has put in black and white sound and earthy wisdom from God's word on how to joyfully persevere in ministry for the long term. I can only thank him for writing it and encourage others in ministry to read it!

PAUL BRENNAN
Location Pastor of the Tron Church, Glasgow

Resilient is full of honest realism, written to Pastors (church leaders) who have 'signed up for hardship and sacrifice'.

Using the timeless truths of 2 Timothy, John shows how it is possible to be resilient, to persevere in ministry, though the challenges and pressures are huge. A sense of God's call to the work is foundational, the right mindset is vital. Resilience is only possible through daily dependence on the grace of God, living in anticipation of the crown of righteousness for the one who labours faithfully. *Resilient* is also a book for our particular times, for those ministering to 'a society in love with itself', the advice is summarised as 'Be sensible. Be sacrificial. Be evangelistic. Be thorough.' This book will be of great help to church leaders, to all who teach God's word and pastor His people and to those who support those who do so.

JULIA JONES
Director of Women's courses at London Seminary and
supporting missionaries with Grace Baptist Mission

At a time of growing ministerial obstacles and opposition, challenges and critics, pastors and Christian workers need to catch a vision for what ministry over the long-haul looks like. How will they persevere? How will they remain faithful? What truths, insights, and encouragements will promote tough-minded endurance when much from within and without might entice them to call it quits? John Benton's *Resilient* provides much needed discussion both of the challenges ministers now face, along with insightful reflections on what is needed to keep on. Benton, a seasoned, experienced pastor himself, walks the reader through 2 Timothy, providing a storehouse of inducements for faithful ministry in the midst of a fallen and broken culture. Included also are many beautiful vignettes from the lives and experiences of those who have walked similar paths and found in God their strength and hope. For encouragement to stay the course, to receive our Lord's 'well done' in the end, I strongly commend this wise, winsome, and inspiring book.

BRUCE A. WARE

T. Rupert and Lucille Coleman Professor of Christian Theology
The Southern Baptist Theological Seminary

How do we keep going in ministry when there seems to be so much against us? Most of us find the reality of ministry to be so much harder than we had expected. Many of us frequently ask ourselves whether we should just give up. In this book John Benton shows how we can develop real resilience for ministry by learning from Paul's letter to a struggling church leader. John combines careful study of 2 Timothy with the wisdom of years of experience on the frontline of church ministry. This is an incredibly helpful, realistic and faith-boosting read for all in ministry, whether you have been soldiering on for many years or are just starting out.

BART ERLEBACH

Associate Vicar at Emmanuel Church, Tolworth, London

JOHN BENTON

Resilient

How 2 Timothy
Teaches us to Bounce Back
in Christian Leadership

CHRISTIAN
FOCUS

Copyright © John Benton 2018

paperback ISBN 978-1-5271-0210-1
epub ISBN 978-1-5271-0251-4
mobi ISBN 978-1-5271-0252-1

First published in 2018
by
Christian Focus Publications Ltd,
Geanies House, Fearn, Ross-shire
IV20 1TW, Scotland
www.christianfocus.com

A CIP catalogue record for this book is available from the British Library.

Cover design by Rubner Durais

Printed and bound by
Bell & Bain, Glasgow.

CONTENTS

Dedication

To all those young, old and yet to come,
privileged to be about the great work
of preaching and teaching
God's Word in God's world at God's call.

I get knocked down, but I get up again
You are never gonna keep me down.

'I get knocked down'
Chumbawamba, 1997

In the clearing stands a boxer
And a fighter by his trade
And he carries the reminders
Of every glove that laid him down
Or cut him 'til he cried out
In his anger and his shame
'I am leaving! I am leaving!'
But the fighter still remains

'The Boxer'
Paul Simon, 1970

Then some Jews came from Antioch and Iconium and won the
crowd over. They stoned Paul and dragged him outside the city,
thinking he was dead. But after the disciples had gathered round
him, he got up and went back into the city. The next day he and
Barnabas left for Derbe.

Acts 14:19-20

Introduction

To be a church leader is the greatest possible privilege. It is a huge honour. To be genuinely called to be a church leader means that God trusts you. He trusts you with the twin treasures of His truth and His church. Christ believes He can rely upon you to be faithful to declare His gospel and to keep safe His bride.

To complete that God-given task is an achievement of real substance. The apostle Paul's words at the end of his second letter to Timothy, as he faces martyrdom and, therefore, the conclusion of his ministry, both stir us and challenge us: 'I have fought the good fight, I have finished the race, I have kept the faith. Now there is in store for me the crown of righteousness...' (2 Tim. 4:7-8). His life's work has come to a successful conclusion. He has done well.

But the road from Damascus to his glorious destination was tough. Though experiencing many joys, at times he had been in despair. On a couple of occasions in his letters Paul lists some of his sufferings as a Christian leader, and those lists frighten the life out of most of us (1 Cor. 4:9-13;

2 Cor. 11:23-29). Yet he lasted the course. He went the distance. He proved resilient in the ministry. It had been an uphill task. But he had not given up. He had not had to give up. He had seen it through to the blessing of God's church right down to the present day.

The men left standing

Some time ago the Evangelical Ministry Assembly organised by The Proclamation Trust, which takes place in London for a few days every summer, began in a striking way. All who attend are involved in Christian ministry in some way. As the first session got under way, we were all invited to stand up. There must have been getting on for a thousand people there. Then, after welcoming us all, the man in charge of the session spoke again. Those who had been in ministry for five years or less were asked to sit down. A large section of the audience retook their seats. Then those who had been in ministry for ten years or less were told to do the same. Then those fifteen years or less. And so it went on. By the time we got to those who had lasted in ministry for thirty-five years or more, there were just a handful of men left standing.

As I contemplated that memorable spectacle, my mind went back to those I had known when I started out as a church leader, who were not there. Some, of course, the Lord has called home to glory. Some had reached retirement age. Some just didn't happen to be at the EMA that year. But there were a lot who, for less happy reasons, were simply no longer in ministry. Some, facing the trials of being a church leader, had decided that it was not really their calling. Some had just found the going too hard for them and their families and had taken other employment, while still going on with the Lord. And there were many others, a few of whom had at one time been headline-name conference speakers, who had crashed out of leadership altogether. Some have even walked out on Christ. Contemplating these things made the fact that there were those left standing seem all the more remarkable. These were leaders who lasted.

What was it about those men left standing? Was it just that God's providence had been extremely kind to them? Or was it that they had learned some very important lessons? The answer was that it is probably a combination of both. The lessons we learn do play a part. They do help us to stand.

At the crossroads

Guard the Gospel was the title of the late John Stott's superb Bible Speaks Today commentary on 2 Timothy.[1] That phrase can rightly be seen as summarising the main theme of Paul's letter as he writes to encourage the younger Christian leader to uphold God's truth in his work.

But, of course, a prerequisite to Timothy guarding the gospel is that he perseveres in gospel ministry. If he drops out as a Christian leader, he is not going to be there to do the vital job of protecting the truth. And, as we read 2 Timothy, we see that Paul is aware that Timothy is pretty near the edge. That's the scenario Paul's letter addresses, it seems. The young leader appears to be suffering a crisis; he is at a crossroads. Will he carry on in ministry or not?

1. John R. W. Stott, *Guard the Gospel: The Message of 2 Timothy* (IVP, 1973).

The signs are there. We are first alerted to this by Paul's prayers. Paul is praying for Timothy 'night and day' and 'constantly' (1:3). That sounds urgent. He goes on to mention Timothy's tears (1:4). Maybe that refers to Timothy weeping at their last parting (perhaps Acts 20:37?). But it shows that Paul recognised that Timothy was something of a sensitive soul who felt things acutely and it might well indicate that Paul imagined that Timothy was a leader who was weeping as he wrote. Paul is going to insist that Timothy travels to see him in prison in Rome (2 Tim. 1:4; 4:9f). We suspect that this request for him to come had more to it than merely Paul's comfort.

In his discouragement Timothy is neglecting his ministry gift (1:6). There is evidence that fear was getting the upper hand in his life (1:7). And Paul feels he has to challenge him about being ashamed of the gospel (1:8).

Why was Timothy struggling?

The Christian ministry is not easy. There are many reasons why we might struggle. I recently carried out a small survey among thirty pastors at a Christian conference. Some had been in ministry a short time; others were old hands. There were ten questions covering a variety of matters. But among the questions was, 'What has made you most feel like giving up in ministry?' Here are some of the answers they gave: 'A sense of helplessness'; 'Myself'; 'Lack of response and growth in the church'; 'Opposition from fellow elders'; 'A sense of isolation'. These things should come as no surprise to us. We are in a battle.

What was Timothy's particular, current battle about? Why was he at a crossroads? It is not completely clear. But reading around the New Testament, we can find at least seven reasons as to why Timothy might have been struggling with doubt and discouragement:

1. He did not enjoy the best of health —1 Timothy 5:23.
2. He seems to have been naturally prone to fear, even of other Christians—1 Corinthians 16:10.
3. He was young and inexperienced. Paul was aware that people tended to look down on him. Perhaps he easily told himself, 'I'm no good'—1 Timothy 4:12.
4. There were a number of pernicious false teachers who were damaging the churches (1 Tim. 1:3; 2 Tim. 2:17; 3:6-8; 3:13), which is always upsetting for faithful men.
5. Generally, it was a difficult period for the cause of Christ and the churches. It seems that many people were deserting the faith (2 Tim. 1:15; 4:10). That must have been very discouraging.
6. Paul himself is about to depart this life. That was a worry. What would happen after he had gone (2 Tim. 4:6)?
7. On top of all this, there was persecution to be faced (2 Tim. 3:12; 4:14). Depending on how we date the book of Hebrews, Timothy either had already or would in the future spend time in prison himself (Heb. 13:23).

Putting all these things together, we can understand why Timothy might be finding that being a Christian leader was very difficult. He was on the brink. And so Paul writes to Timothy.

There are dark days, fiery darts, blows to the head and to the heart, stabs in the back, seductions and temptations—

all manner of pitfalls and punches that bruise, bash, scar, and dent us and our pride. We can't avoid them. Like it or not, we are in the arena. The spiritual battle rages around us. But resilience is the ability to bounce back. These days, to be resilient carries the idea of simply being tough and hard-wearing. But the word *resile*, from which the noun *resilience* is derived, means to rebound, to recoil, to recover form and position elastically. We are not to be elastic but rigid and unbending concerning gospel truth. But when it comes to the spiritual contest, we need to be able to roll with the punches. Like Paul at Lystra, though we may get knocked down, we need to be able to get up again and carry on (Acts 14:19, 20). In 2 Corinthians 4:9, Paul speaks of his experience in ministry as being 'struck down, but not destroyed'—he gets up again. Resilience, though not a New Testament word, is closely related to the idea of resurrection, which very definitely is.[2] That's our kind of toughness.

We need resilience as Christians. We need an extra dose of resilience as Christian leaders. Timothy is wavering; but Paul is not. What does he have to teach the young man? What does he have to say to those of us in ministry today? We are going to approach 2 Timothy with that question in mind. That will be our constant focus.

So, this little book is not meant to be a full commentary on 2 Timothy. Rather, we are coming to it wearing a particular pair of spectacles. We address its different sections with one question. We want to see what it has to say

---

2. The Greek for resurrection—*anastasis*—literally means 'stand up again'.

about finding strength, recovering from discouragement and keeping going as a Christian leader. That means that some of the purple passages and important doctrinal truths of which Paul writes will hardly be mentioned. We will skate quickly over them. On another occasion they deserve and would repay deep study. But we will just skim the surface. Think of it like this: we are not going to sit down in the restaurant to enjoy ourselves, we are just driving through the takeaway area to pick up what we need.

Exercise for those in ministry

In this introduction a list was given of some of the problems which Timothy was facing and may have contributed to his apparent crisis which Paul addresses in 2 Timothy.

- Make a list of seven things which you find most difficult about ministry life.
- Name each one of these in prayer to God and lay them at His feet.

1
A Vulnerable Man Called by God

Paul, an apostle of Christ Jesus by the will of God, according to the promise of life that is in Christ Jesus, to Timothy, my dear son: Grace, mercy and peace from God the Father and Christ Jesus our Lord. (2 Tim. 1:1-2)

———————————

The boy was around fifteen years old. As an unconverted teenager, who had begun to be interested in Christian things, he was taken by some friends to Westminster Chapel in London, to a Sunday evening service at which Dr Martyn Lloyd-Jones was preaching. The place was packed. The teenager and his friends sat high up, at the back of the building. The preacher looked very small and distant in his black gown. But what a great impact! The young lad found it was an amazing experience. The service gripped him. The gospel was preached and it all seemed to finish when it had hardly begun. Time had somehow stood still. The boy had tasted eternity. God was there. It made a deep and lasting impression.

Let's start thinking about ministry by stating something completely obvious but which could not be more important. Paul is going to be encouraging Timothy in ministry and is in ministry himself—as an apostle. Here's the wood which we mustn't miss for the trees. **All ministry needs to come from people who truly know God.** Even the Pharisees handled Scripture—at some levels very learnedly. But they did not know God. Dr Lloyd-Jones did. Ministry which is really ministry will only emerge from a vital relationship with God.

As Paul begins his letter—in a slightly stiff and formal way it has to be said—to his young friend Timothy (we will talk about that in a moment), he states himself to be 'Paul, an apostle of Christ Jesus by the will of God'. The underlying truth here is that Paul can write so freely of the will of God concerning himself because he knows God. Later he will write: 'I know whom I have believed' (1:12). He met Him first on the road to Damascus—the risen Lord Jesus Christ, God the Son in scarred but glorified human flesh. That encounter dramatically and profoundly changed Paul. He met Christ, whom to know is life eternal (John 17:3). From then on he entered into a personal experience of the 'life that is in Christ Jesus' (1:1). Yes, at present that is a life lived by faith. We see 'through a glass, darkly'. We do not yet know the promised eternal fullness of it. But we do know it. And the life we know is, in Henry Scougal's great phrase, 'the life of God in the soul of man'.[1] Ministry is meant to be the loving and powerful overflow of that inner life of Spirit and truth to those around us.

---

1. Henry Scougal, *The Life of God in the Soul of Man* (1677).

We know God

As we contemplate the work of ministry for God in a fallen world, this is the place at which we must begin. If we have surrendered our lives to Jesus Christ in repentance and faith, then we have entered into a true knowledge of, and a relationship with, God. Think of all the potential which that carries with it. Sometimes, amid our problems, we forget that. More than likely Timothy had forgotten it too. That was part of his crisis. But Paul comes in quickly and affectionately to speak of Timothy as 'my dear son'. Spiritually, Timothy is of the same family as Paul. Paul is going to go on to assure Timothy that he sees marks of true faith in him (1:5). Timothy might not have had that Damascus Road experience enjoyed by Paul. But, as he believes the good news, he too knows God as his Father through Christ Jesus our Lord.

As we noted, Paul opens the letter rather formally: 'Paul, an apostle… To Timothy'. In doing so he signals to Timothy that ministry is no game. There is a weightiness, an importance about it, that could not be more profound. Timothy, along with all of us as pastors and preachers, is dealing with eternal realities. We stand at the parting of the ways between the roads to heaven and hell to direct lost souls. We are serving the purposes of Almighty God. Yet, knowing Timothy's current troubled state, Paul's introduction mixes that weightiness with the warmth and humanity of calling him 'my dear son'.

A man ministering out of a deep relationship with God has access to God and to His power. Of course, many years ago, that young teenager I mentioned earlier who visited Westminster Chapel was myself. It was a night never to be forgotten which started me on the road to finding Christ.

We may not have the gifts of the late Dr Lloyd-Jones, but we know the same God. What an encouragement that is! We may be small, vulnerable people, but we know God. Having made that foundational point, let's move on.

The opening sentences of Paul's letters often contain telling phrases, even the heart of his message in a nutshell. We can look upon 1:1-2 as something of an initial summary of some of the crucial items which are on Paul's agenda for Timothy. There are three key concepts which leap out of the text related to resilience in Christian life and ministry. These are: the will of God (1:1), the promise of God (1:1) and the grace of God (1:2).

The will of God

Paul's mention of the will of God is related to his own call into ministry: 'Paul, an apostle of Christ Jesus by the will of God'. Not only do we know God, we have been called into the ministry by God. We are not called to be apostles in the way that Paul was. Those unique witnesses to the resurrection of the Lord Jesus Christ were foundational to the church and belong to the initial years of church history. But, though we are just ordinary pastors and preachers, if we are legitimately in post, then we have been called by God too. We have been appointed to our work by His will.

I spoke with a pastor not long ago whose deacons took a dislike to him after some years of faithful and fruitful service. They wanted to get rid of him. It later emerged that one of them had even skewed the accounts to give the impression that giving had dropped. This was cited as evidence that the church was no longer behind the pastor and benefitting from his ministry. I can't explain why such things happen in a Christian congregation, except to say that the devil is real. But the trouble having now passed, the pastor said, 'John, during those days, if it had not been that I felt so sure that God had called me, I could never have stood up to preach.' A solid call to the ministry brings strength during difficult times. What constitutes this call?

As Paul gives his farewell address to the elders of the local church in Ephesus on the beach at Miletus, he charges them to 'keep watch over yourselves and all the flock of which the Holy Spirit has made you overseers' (Acts 20:28). Notice, these church leaders did not appoint themselves. Nor were they simply appointed by the church. God the Holy Spirit had a hand in it.

How is the Holy Spirit involved? There are two things to say. *Firstly*, in a genuine call to ministry, the Holy Spirit puts a persistent burning desire into a man's heart to serve the Lord's people out of love for Christ and love for them (1 Tim. 3:1). When a man examines himself and digs deep into what is prompting him in the direction of ministry, he is bound to find some things that shouldn't be there. He is a fallen sinner, like all of us. But nevertheless as he sifts through his motives, he does find a sincere concern for Christ and His cause and even an inner pressure from the Spirit to serve. He knows that he can't be at peace unless he offers himself to the work. He often feels a 'fire' inside himself as he looks at Scripture and a compelling message he must deliver (Jer. 20:9).

Secondly, the call of God is seen, in that the Holy Spirit has worked gifts and graces, the Christian maturity of godliness, faith and wisdom, in a man which the church is able to recognise as meeting the requirements of character for leadership. Paul lists these in 1 Timothy 3:1-7 and Titus 1:5-9. The church perceives that, although the man is not perfect, still he shows clear signs that the Holy Spirit has been shaping his character to make a leader for God's church.

No two calls to the ministry are precisely the same. Many of us know other providences and experiences which confirmed our calling in addition to the two marks I have mentioned. But these two are the essentials of calling to ministry. And if those essentials are there, then it is the Holy Spirit who has appointed us to leadership. It is just as much God's will for us to be pastors as it was for Paul to be an apostle.

Knowing that we are called by God contributes enormously to resilience and tenacity in ministry. Why was that pastor I mentioned earlier able to preach despite unfair opposition? Why was it that Paul was able to suffer so much and yet not throw in the towel? It was because, before everything else, he knew that God had placed him in the work. He had not thrust himself into post. God had put him there and, therefore, he knew he was in the right place, at the right time, doing the right thing with his life. He knew, also, that because God had called him to it, God would equip him to do it.

When faced with the stresses and strains of ministry, it is worth more than gold to know that it is God's will for you to be in ministry. Dr Lloyd-Jones used to say something like, 'No one should go into ministry unless they know it is impossible for them to do anything else.' Some have thought him rather harsh for taking such a line. But, in actual fact, his words are full of kindness and wisdom. To know that you are called by God will give you a strength and certainty (mixed with humility) which nothing else can. It is his knowledge that it is God's will for him to be in the work with which Paul begins his letter. It is a key to resilience.

The promise of God

The call of God to ministry and the promise of God go together, of course. But it is worth reflecting that when we suffer, it is not only helpful to know that we are in God's will, but also to know that our suffering serves a bigger purpose. If it doesn't serve any greater good, then what is the point of suffering? It will appear useless. We might as well give up.

Paul has been called to the work of an apostle 'according to the promise of the life that is in Christ Jesus' (1:1). He is sent—and, of course, the word 'apostle' means one who has been sent—to proclaim the gospel of Christ, the good news that promises eternal life through repentance and faith.

In her book reviewing the work and findings of many secular psychology academics concerning what makes a resilient person, Kirsten Birkett quotes research which says: 'Holding a set of core beliefs that are positive about oneself and one's role in the world, and that few things can shatter' is of great importance.[2]

When ministry is difficult, we are suffering in order to bring eternal life to lost men and women, boys and girls. Eternal life is God's promise to all who believe. We are spending our lives, in cooperation with God, on the most important rescue mission in history. The commission the Lord gave to Paul applies to us too: 'I am sending you to them to open their eyes and turn them from darkness to light, and from the power of Satan to God, so that they may receive forgiveness of sins and a place among those who are sanctified by faith in me' (Acts 26:17, 18). Our work of making known God's promise could not be more worthwhile.

Christ's death and resurrection which we preach, not only mean that death and hell are swallowed up in God's victory on behalf of ourselves and all who believe, but that same good news has been, and continues to be, the inspiration of much loving care and many good deeds in this present world. As God has so loved us in Christ, so we are inspired to love others. The beginnings of education, hospitals, prison reform and so many charities across the world have their roots in 'the promise of life' which we preach.

So, at both levels, temporal and eternal, we who preach and lead the churches are about a good work. We are not wasting our energy. We are not engaged on a fool's errand. We have reason to be eminently positive about

---

2. Kirsten Birkett, *Resilience: A Spiritual Project*, Latimer Studies (Latimer Trust, 2016), page 22.

ourselves and our role in the world. The promise of God is, therefore, another key that unlocks resilience for us.

The world scoffs at gospel ministers. We are looked upon as misguided men. We might be tempted to compare ourselves with old school or university friends who have 'made it' in life, now commanding large salaries and jet-setting lifestyles. We spend hours in the study. We spend hours in prayer. We visit homes and the hospitals and the hospices. And sometimes we ask, 'Am I wasting my time?' No! We are not wasting our time because the promise of God stands and will stand when this present world, its wisdom, wealth and attractions, are long gone.

The grace of God

Having given his formal introduction involving God's will and God's promise, Paul both proclaims and prays the grace of God upon his dear son in the faith, Timothy: 'Grace, mercy, and peace from God the Father and Christ Jesus our Lord' (1:2).

Christian leaders have been called in God's will to do the work of making known God's promise to mankind and looking after those who believe. But we need to know this too: our God is not some grim taskmaster who presents us with a gigantic project and then simply walks away and leaves us to get on with it while demanding the best results. This is the devil's caricature of God. If we allow this twisted portrait to influence us, we will soon walk away when trouble comes in ministry. Who would want to labour long, to spend and be spent for such a thoughtless, hard-hearted boss?

But God is not our 'boss'. He is our loving Father. He has grace for us. This grace is one of the primary sources of strength for those in the ministry (see 2:1), and we are going to concentrate on it more fully later in the book. But Paul mentions it in his first paragraph: 'Grace, mercy, and peace from God the Father and Christ Jesus our Lord' (1:2).

We note that grace always comes first for the apostle. As in all his Epistles, right from the beginning, Paul puts grace upfront and centre.[3] So we will note a few things about grace here, even though we will explore it a little more fully later. Grace, mercy and peace?

- *First*, God's *grace* is His lovingly favourable attitude towards us. Though we ought to be objects of God's displeasure and wrath because of our sin, in Christ Jesus we come into His permanent approval, affection and kindness. Whether we have a good day or a bad day, He still loves us and treasures us. Whether we triumph or trip up, He is still on our side.
- *Second*, this favour of God which we enjoy is not according to our deserving or achieving. It comes to us in Christ Jesus through pure *mercy*. It is not according to our works. It is not earned by anything that proceeds from our heredity, our hearts, heads or hands. It is not related to who our people were or our exam results. It is not dependent on how hard we pray,

3. Romans 1:7; 1 Corinthians 1:3; 2 Corinthians 1:2; Galatians 1:3; Ephesians 1:2; Philippians 1:2; Colossians 1:2; 1 Thessalonians 1:1; 2 Thessalonians 1:2; 1 Timothy 1:2; 2 Timothy 1:2; Titus 1:4; Philemon 3.

how many people we visit, how well we prepare or preach our sermons. In Christ, God the Father is for us—always—by pure mercy.

- *Third*, this permanent attitude of warm and loving favour is translated into action. He brings us into true *peace*: peace with Himself which is the genuine *shalom*. He forgives all our sins through the Cross of Christ. He works all things for our ultimate good (Rom. 8:28). When we suffer, this is not a sign that God has left us. It is rather that God is working in a different way to bless us, make us more like Jesus and give us the privilege of being rewarded for glorifying Him through sacrifice.

What a thing is the grace of God! It is an enormously effective key to getting a handle on difficulties and bouncing back.

As God's men, when we suffer in ministry, we should think of ourselves as akin to Old Testament Joseph. Betrayed by his brothers into slavery, framed by Potiphar's wife, forgotten by a compatriot he had helped, imprisoned beneath the ground: yet God was with him and all was being worked for good. Even what others meant for evil, God meant for good (Gen. 50:20). Joseph was a man under God's grace. And in Christ Jesus, so are we. So don't despair.

As God's men, under pressure, we sometimes fall. The Old Testament hero Samson sinned catastrophically in a way I hope we never shall. He lost his strength to Delilah's scheming. And yet he bounced back to destroy the Philistines in his dying. He found resilience. Matthew

Henry draws the lesson: 'What has been lost by sin may be regained by penitent prayer.' That is true for us too, because, in Christ Jesus, we are under God's grace. So don't give up on yourself.

There is always a temptation to turn Christianity into a deadly religion of merit and to leave behind the joy of grace. Paul puts God's grace always front and centre and it's our job as Christian leaders to do the same. And the first place to apply that is to ourselves.

Exercise for those in ministry

One of the main themes highlighted in this chapter was that a sense of our being called by God to the ministry can be a great source of strength.

- Think through and write out on a side of A4 paper a short account of your own call to the ministry. What were the turning points which most convinced you of your call?
- Thank God in prayer for your call to serve Him as a pastor / preacher / teacher.

2
Beginning to Build Resilience

I thank God, whom I serve, as my forefathers did, with a clear
conscience, as night and day I constantly remember you in my
prayers. Recalling your tears, I long to see you, so that I may be
filled with joy. I have been reminded of your sincere faith, which
first lived in your grandmother Lois and in your mother Eunice
and, I am persuaded, now lives in you also. For this reason I
remind you to fan into flame the gift of God, which is in you
through the laying on of my hands. For God did not give us a spirit
of timidity, but a spirit of power, of love and of self-discipline.

*   So do not be ashamed to testify about our Lord, or ashamed*
of me his prisoner. But join with me in suffering for the gospel,
by the power of God, who has saved us and called us to a holy
life—not because of anything we have done but because of his
own purpose and grace. This grace was given us in Christ Jesus
before the beginning of time, but has now been revealed through the
appearing of our Saviour, Christ Jesus, who has destroyed death
and has brought life and immortality to light through the gospel.
And of this gospel I was appointed a herald and an apostle and
a teacher. That is why I am suffering as I am. Yet I am not

ashamed, because I know whom I have believed, and am convinced
that he is able to guard what I have entrusted to him for that day.
What you heard from me, keep as the pattern of sound teaching,
with faith and love in Christ Jesus. Guard the good deposit that
was entrusted to you—guard it with the help of the Holy Spirit
who lives in us. (2 Tim. 1:3-14)

His name was Tony. He was married, the father of five children and he worked as a civil servant. He was one of the most tenacious men I ever knew. He was a deacon and then an elder of the church of which I was pastor before he moved on to help lead a church-replanting project in which we were involved. Now he is with the Lord.

But in the mid-1960s—long before I arrived—the church went through a bad time. The congregation had dwindled to just a handful on Sunday evenings. There was often acrimony among members, especially at church meetings. The church building was old and not in a good state of repair. While other churches in the town were thriving, God seemed to have passed this one by. People weren't up for serving in the church, some were leaving and much of what needed to be done by way of administration and practical jobs got left to Tony.

At the same time his wife, Mary, fell into quite serious depression. It was a difficult time. But this man had grit. While other people were jumping ship, Tony said to his wife, 'The harder it gets the more determined I am to stay'. She loved him for it. With God's enabling, he was true to his word. He and a few others carried the church through that very destructive and dark period and later God blessed it in a great way. But, humanly speaking, if it had not been for that resilient man Tony, I'm not sure there would have been a church left for God to bless.

Timothy's friend

As Paul writes to Timothy, it seems clear that Timothy is wobbling. He was not naturally made of the same stuff as my friend Tony. Yet he needed that same tenacity in the struggle in which he was engaged if he was to fulfil his ministry, guard the gospel and be a valiant preacher of the Word in a wayward generation (4:3, 4).

Paul has already made it plain that he looks upon Timothy as his 'dear son' in the faith. Reading Acts, it is not clear whether Timothy had been led to Christ through Paul, with his mother and grandmother's influence, on the apostle's first missionary journey when he preached the gospel in Lystra (Acts 14:8-20), or whether he was already a Christian when Paul first came and Paul just 'adopted' him as his 'dear son' spiritually.

Timothy was from Lystra and it was there that Paul had faced stoning, and was thought dead, though he later recovered. It is this kind of resilience which Christian workers need. We get knocked down, but we get up again.

Paul must have noticed young Timothy and, in need of another companion, when he visited Lystra again on his second missionary journey, he invited him to join his mission team and come with him.

Paul came to Derbe and then to Lystra, where a disciple named Timothy lived, whose mother was a Jewess and a believer but whose father was a Greek. The brothers at Lystra and Iconium spoke well of him. Paul wanted to take him along on the journey, so he circumcised him because of the Jews who lived in the area, for they all knew his father was a Greek. (Acts 16:1-3)

Timothy had earned a good reputation as a keen Christian among the churches, and acceded to Paul's wisdom that he be circumcised so as not to cause any misunderstanding that might divert Jewish folk from listening to the gospel. This showed a commitment and a willingness in Timothy to do whatever was necessary to help the cause of the Lord Jesus.

So an affectionate bond grew up between Paul and Timothy which is very obviously expressed in 1:3-4 of our section. Paul prays urgently and repeatedly for Timothy and he longs to see him so 'that I may be filled with joy'.

It is Paul's deep concern and love for Timothy that becomes a proper platform from which to address Timothy's need to be resilient. Paul's affection for Timothy, expressed in the letter, no doubt encouraged and steadied Timothy. But, more crucially, it is that affection which enabled Timothy to receive what Paul had to say to help him. John Stott writes: 'Such a Christian friendship, including the companionship, the letters and the prayers through which it was expressed, did not fail to have a powerful moulding effect on young Timothy, strengthening and sustaining him in his Christian life and service.'[1]

Why some young pastors give up

Some young men set out in the ministry but do not last long. Sometimes that is due to the fact that they do not

---

1. John R. W. Stott, *Guard the Gospel* (IVP, 1973), page 29.

have the kind of support from an older, wiser friend (or trusted group of mature Christian friends) that Timothy enjoyed. What tends to happen with some young men is something like the following scenario.

They are part of an established local church when they feel the call to ministry. Though they have no place for them on the home team, their church recognises that they have a gift and feels it is right to support them prayerfully and perhaps financially through seminary. But having done that, the church believes that basically it has fulfilled its obligations. Also, at the conclusion of their training, the seminary too, which has been very glad to teach the young man and benefit from the fees which he has paid them, loosens the ties with him. Having seen him through to graduation, they too might think they have done all that is required.

The young seminary graduate then launches forth into the marketplace of churches seeking pastors and eventually lands a position. It is likely that it will be in a location geographically distant from his home town and, anyway, it is now three or four years since he (and his young family?) were really part of their home church. The seminary is now focused on a new batch of students and, apart from a few emails advertising further courses, takes little or no personal interest in him. Besides a few friends of his own age he met at seminary (equally lacking in pastoral experience) with whom he keeps in contact, our young man is cut adrift in a new church he hardly knows and which, although hopefully enthusiastic towards the new man, hardly knows him. The people of the church and their elders are as yet only slightly more than acquaintances. They are not friends to whom he can easily open his heart. What's more, there may even be an element in the congregation that says, 'We pay his salary, and having been trained at Bible college, he should know the answers and not have to ask us.'

Furthermore, the local pastors' fraternal turns out to be a competitive gathering as men ask one another, 'How's your church doing?' Sometimes, it is little more than a stage on which the more successful pastors can smugly display how marvellous their own ministries are, while everyone else feels useless and inept. The rest keep quiet about their real troubles and lack of progress.

And so it is that, when the road of pastoral ministry gets tough, the young man whom we have been considering is on his own. He is out on a limb. He has no one to turn to—except perhaps his wife. And they fret together and feel so inadequate. Without outside help, they lack perspective and things get out of proportion. They tear their hair out alone. And they talk together amid the tears. And eventually another young ministry couple decides they can't take it any longer and resign. They have to do it to save their sanity and their family life. It's a tragedy for them and for the cause of Christ.

If only there had been an older friend who had been through the mill in ministry and to whom the young man had felt confident in turning to amid his troubles, the situation might have been saved. Perhaps it could have been the pastor or a kind elder from his old home church? Perhaps it could have been a humble, gentle and respected senior pastor from the fraternal? If only …

Fortunately for Timothy, as he faced his time of crisis, he had Paul who loved him and looked out for him. So it is that Paul writes to Timothy. And it is very clear from the text that Paul is not on his own ego trip to be a 'mentor' of distinction. He is not out to throw his weight around and show Timothy how great an apostle he is. He writes out of genuine affection and he makes sure that Timothy knows it. It will be Paul's obvious love for Timothy that will open the door of Timothy's heart, so he hears what the apostle has to say to him.

In these verses, Paul begins to intervene and encourage Timothy to stay true. He is aiming to build Timothy's resilience. How does Paul go about that? Let me suggest three things.

Paul appeals to Timothy's sincerity (1:3-5)

Paul is convinced Timothy is a sincere young pastor. He encourages him saying, 'I have been reminded of your sincere faith' (1:5). Timothy was good-hearted. Elsewhere Paul commends him by saying: 'I have no one else like him, who takes a genuine interest in your welfare. For everyone looks out for his own interests, not those of Jesus Christ. But you know that Timothy has proved himself, because as a son with his father he has served with me in the work of the gospel.' (Phil. 2:20-22)

In order to begin to haul Timothy back from the brink of giving up in ministry, Paul is going to appeal to Timothy's sincerity and loyalty. He does this, not so much to directly build resilience, but to stir in Timothy at least the desire not to give up. This, on its own, will not give the strength needed, but it will be a start.

This, it seems, is why Paul now introduces the whole theme of faith being continued down the generations. Paul mentions his own forefathers in this connection (1:3). He then goes on to speak of Timothy's grandmother Lois and mother Eunice with the idea of the baton being carried and passed on in time and in the family. He is subtly encouraging Timothy not to drop the baton.

There were other ways Paul could have done this. But his emphasis in the early verses of this letter is on Timothy's family (1:3-5). This is unusual. Though Paul often mentions all kinds of people in the final greetings of his Epistles, there is nothing parallel with what we have here in the opening verses of a Pauline Epistle anywhere else. Generally speaking, he mentions the recipient(s) at the beginning, but otherwise he leaves referencing others to the end of the Epistle. However, here, having cited his own ancestors (1:3), he then goes on to talk about Timothy's grandmother and his mother (1:5). They, too, were sincere believers. He is going to return to these two women later in chapter 3. But why does he mention them here as he opens the letter?

I would suggest that Paul's strategy is to stir Timothy's sincerity and loyalty with the implied question, 'Are you going to be the one to drop the baton so faithfully carried by those so dear to you?' Timothy's faith is at a low ebb. Perhaps to challenge him immediately about the need for grit and determination would be asking too much. So Paul starts with people Timothy cherishes—his Christian family.

Paul is implying, 'If you gave up, think what it would do to your mum and your granny.' At the same time, mentioning how he, Paul, has served God 'as my forefathers did', he is setting a precedent, which he hopes Timothy will take seriously. Timothy's ministry is in the balance. Will he carry on or not? Timothy is weighing up the negatives and positives. Paul is trying to put some more weight into the positive side of the scales.

As he contemplates the possibility of turning his back on ministry, hopefully it will bring him to conclude: 'I don't want to let them down!' It will help him get a grip and decide, with God's help, to keep going for Christ.

Sometimes, resilience in the Christian life emerges first of all out of loyalty to those we love in Christ. In Psalm 73, Asaph, battling with doubts because of the prosperity of the wicked, takes himself in hand with similar thoughts. If he had expressed all his immediate feelings about how useless it currently appeared to serve God, 'I would have betrayed ... your children' (Ps. 73:15). He won't do it. Our determination should come out of our commitment to Christ. But sometimes we slip so low that we need a step up to get back to that ideal attitude. Thoughts of those who are close to us and who love us in Christ can provide us with such a step.

I think it was something of this that gave grit to Tony, whose story I mentioned at the start of this chapter. How come he was resolved that 'the harder things get the more determined I am to stay'? I think his back story may help us to understand.

Tony originally came to our town as a boy during WWII. London was being bombed and children were evacuated from the capital and placed with families in less dangerous places around the country. Tony came as an evacuee to our town and was taken in by Pastor John Peters, the then incumbent of our church. Pastor Peters had a long ministry at the church spanning both the World Wars of the twentieth century. There, in John Peters' home, he experienced the kindness and love of the pastor's family and saw first-hand that man's godliness and hard work for the Lord and his church. John Peters won a special place in Tony's heart. I think that at least some of Tony's determination to carry the church through the low times was born out of a deep affection for the man who had persevered in ministry and had looked after him. I can imagine Tony saying to himself, 'I can't let him down. I can't let the church he worked so hard to maintain go to scrap!'

Paul is hoping to stir similar sentiments in Timothy. This is where he begins to build resilience. And, of course, Paul's subtle reminder of Timothy's believing mother and grandmother is wrapped up in his night and day prayers for his young friend.

As we face our darkest times in ministry, it is good to remind ourselves of Christian role models, friends and family who have been good to us. That desire not to let them down can give us a toehold when we feel we can't cling on any longer. Perhaps we will be able to remember their testimonies, the dark times the Lord brought them through, and so be inspired to remain faithful.

Paul points to God's capability (1:6-12)

Paul now moves on to direct Timothy beyond himself. He wants Timothy to look to God.

It is quite a commonplace observation that confident people, assured of their own abilities and effectiveness, usually make more resilient people. Their project collapses and somehow they are not deterred. Believing in themselves, they get up and have another go. We tend to call them 'can do' people. They seem to have a built-in optimism that they can manage all life's challenges. 'Problems are there to be solved!' is their attitude. They can keep going.

But others who generally lack confidence in themselves and who perceive the world as difficult and threatening, find it much more problematic to persevere. Rather, when they get knocked down, they tend to stay on the floor. They tell themselves, 'I'm useless' or 'I'm going to fail anyway, so I might as well give up now and not waste any more time.'

Being optimistic about oneself correlates with being a person who is naturally more able to bounce back. The trouble is, of course, that many, perhaps most of us, are not like that. Certainly Timothy wasn't. So what's the answer?

Paul's answer is to point to the power and capability of God. In this section, 1:6-12, Paul is reminding Timothy that, though we may not have reason to be optimistic about our own powers, we have every reason to be optimistic about our God and what He can do. We may not have the resources in ourselves, but God is still there for us. That is the basis for our resilience and perseverance. God Himself wants to be involved in the work. 'So don't give up, but stir yourself!' is what Paul is saying. Pick up the things you have let drop. The direction of this paragraph can be sketched under three subheadings: exhortation, demonstration, conviction.

Exhortation

> *For this reason I remind you to fan into flame the gift of God, which is in you through the laying on of my hands. For God did not give us a spirit of timidity, but of power, of love and of self-discipline. So do not be ashamed to testify about our Lord, or ashamed of me his prisoner. But join me in suffering for the gospel, by the power of God. (1:6-8)*

Paul's reasoning goes like this: on the basis of your sincere faith, I know you are a true believer and therefore you have within you not only particular ministry gifts but the gift of the Holy Spirit Himself (1:7). You are not on your own, but indwelt by Him who is the power of God, so don't be afraid or ashamed (1:8). Join me in suffering. Get back into the work. The Lord will enable you and give you strength to endure.

Paul is calling for belief, but not self-belief. We are to believe in the power of the Holy Spirit to sustain us and use us. That allusion to the presence of the Holy Spirit with Timothy is important. He is the Spirit of power, love and self-control. Paul will come back to it in 1:14 and so will we.

The call to join Paul in suffering for the gospel by the power of God (the Holy Spirit) would have had special resonance for Timothy. A native of Lystra, as we have already noted, Timothy would have known first-hand of Paul being stoned and left for dead outside the city. But in God's power and goodness, he rose again—in a sense rather like Christ (Acts 14:19, 20).

And God had gone on to use the 'risen' Paul mightily. Later, Timothy had joined Paul on his second missionary journey. It was the venture of faith which took the gospel into Europe for the first time. He would have been around and known first-hand how, in Philippi, Paul and Silas had been suffering for the gospel in prison, but how God sent the earthquake and used it to save the jailer and his family.

'So join me in suffering for the gospel, by the power of God,' Paul says. Our eyes might naturally be drawn to the word 'suffering'. But Paul's experiences showed the great possibilities of God's power being at work in such circumstances.

As we are prepared to suffer, the gospel will spread and the church will grow. 'I tell you the truth, said the Lord Jesus, unless a grain of wheat falls into the ground and dies, it remains only a single seed. But if it dies it produces many seeds.' (John 12:24)

Demonstration

Timothy is encouraged to join Paul in suffering for the gospel by the power of God 'who has saved us and called us to a holy life—not because of anything we have done but because of his own purpose and grace. This grace was given us in Christ Jesus before the beginning of time, but has now been revealed through the appearing of our Saviour, Christ Jesus, who has destroyed death and has brought life and immortality to light through the gospel.' (1:9-10)

These sentences are meant to demonstrate two things to Timothy. They show Timothy both ultimate safety and almighty power.

When we face suffering, we like to know that we are going to be safe in the end, that there is light at the end of the tunnel. The power of God means that we are safe. He has 'saved us' (1:9). Note the past tense. It's done and dusted. We can afford to take risks. We are saved.

That salvation is by grace, 'not because of anything we have done' (1:9). It was given us before we were even born (1:9). We did nothing to earn it and, because we did nothing to earn it, we can't undo it. We are safe. Furthermore, the security of that salvation has been demonstrated by Jesus' resurrection from the dead (1:10). Suppose the worst happens and in suffering for Christ we are killed. So what? Jesus was killed, but He rose again and His resurrection guarantees that we will rise too. We cannot be lost. The light at the end of the tunnel is shining. It burst out of the empty tomb on Easter morning.

But more than safety, think of the magnitude of what God's power has already achieved in the gospel. The grace of God was shown in Christ 'who has destroyed death and has brought life and immortality to light through the gospel' (1:10). If in His grace the power of God has done that, then God is perfectly capable of sustaining us through any troubles we might suffer for Him. So trust Him. Don't back off. Keep going. Who knows what He can do through you?

Conviction

Here Paul underlines what he has been saying by expressing his own personal conviction. His testimony is one of certainty that God will not let him (or us) down. 'And of this gospel I was appointed a herald and an apostle and a teacher. That is why I am suffering as I am. Yet, I am not ashamed, because I know whom I have believed, and am convinced that he is able to guard what I have entrusted to him for that day.' (1:11-12)

What is it that Paul has entrusted to God? Is it his gospel work? Is it his life? I believe it is both. It is all that Paul has given his life for in the cause of God. Preaching the gospel in a fallen world always attracts trouble. That's par for the course. 'But in the light of the power of God demonstrated in the gospel,' Paul is saying, 'I'm persuaded that my life and ministry is not in vain. On the Day of Judgment, the only day that counts in the end, I am convinced that my life will not have been wasted but will be shown to have been more than worthwhile. I have entrusted all that I am and devoted myself to the service of the gospel. I will not be the loser! God will ensure that. So join me!'

Resilience for the Christian minister is not about having a buoyant, upbeat personality. It is not about being confident of our abilities. Those things can so easily be punctured and, in my experience, very often they are.

Resilience is about faith. It is about being confident in God's capabilities. And that means there is hope for all of us, 'for nothing is impossible with God' (Luke 1:37). 'Now to him who is able to do immeasurably more than all we ask or imagine, according to his power that is at work within us, to him be the glory.' (Eph. 3:20). That loyal sticking with the faith of your family, Timothy, is not foolish. God is able!

Paul focuses on Timothy's responsibility

So what is Timothy being urged to do? What is the responsibility that Paul wants Timothy to take up afresh and re-engage with? Clarity about our primary responsibility as ministers may well help us in persevering. We are not called to do everything. However, we must guard the gospel. We are called to preserve and promote the gospel. 'What you heard from me, keep as the pattern of sound teaching, with faith and love in Christ Jesus. Guard the good deposit that was entrusted to you—guard it with the help of the Holy Spirit who lives in us.' (1:13-14)

Here is the bottom line of ministry. The world and the church need sound teaching—teaching that will make the spiritually sick healthy again. The context here, if you remember, is that there is much false teaching about. Where do we find sound teaching? It comes from the apostles of Christ. Paul, as an apostle, tells Timothy to preserve and promote 'what you heard from me.' This is the pattern of sound teaching which produces 'faith and love', spiritual life and health, wherever it takes root. This was the vital matter.

I have heard it said rightly that, despite our fears, persecution cannot destroy God's church. But what we need to realise is that false teaching can! Paul was aware of this. That is why Timothy must take seriously this sacred trust that has been handed to him to keep and teach the gospel. So don't be discouraged. Those hours in the study seeking prayerfully to understand the Scriptures could not be more important.

But Paul then quickly reminds his 'dear son' that he is not on his own or without help in this vital task. 'Guard it with the help of the Holy Spirit who lives in us.' (1:14) The Holy Spirit, He through whom the power of God is exercised—even in raising Jesus from the dead[2]—is with Timothy and in Timothy. He is the Spirit 'of power, of love and of self-discipline' (1:7). This great Helper can turn our weakness to advantage and make our feeble efforts gloriously effective. Jesus performed His own ministry in the power of the Spirit (Luke 4:14) and gave that same Spirit to the church on the day of Pentecost.

And the Spirit loves to use those who, in themselves, are ill-equipped. On the day of Pentecost what good would twelve country bumpkins from Galilee be able to do for people, given the politically astute and well-educated leadership of the Jews who dominated the life and Temple worship of Jerusalem? Yet, as the Spirit came, those twelve apostles caused a mighty spiritual explosion with their witness for Christ. We, as weak, failing Timothys, need to remember such things.

A few years ago something happened which proved a precious illustration to me of the Holy Spirit's work. Each Christmas time we ran a 'scratch nativity' at the church for the children of the area. The children would come at 6pm and, 'from scratch', rehearse a little Christmas play—and the parents would come at 7pm to watch the performance. There was just one hour. It was always a

---

2. Romans 1:4.

close-run thing as to whether we could get ready in time without the whole thing falling apart.

As part of the production, there would always be a few traditional Christmas carols for everyone to sing and usually I would strum along amateurishly on the guitar while someone else would do their best on the piano.

However, this particular year something very memorable took place. Attending our congregation when he is not touring the world is a man who is the principal flautist of one of the greatest orchestras in the UK. His wife became a Christian at the church some time ago and he comes to church with her. I will call him Harry (not his real name) and I will not tell you which orchestra. As I was welcoming the parents and they began to enter the building for our 'scratch nativity', there was Harry with his wife. Cheekily, I found myself saying to him, 'Have you got your flute with you, Harry?' 'Yes, I have,' he said. 'Would you mind helping us with the Christmas Carols?' I asked. (What a ludicrous thing to say!) To my surprise he said, 'Do you know, I've been rehearsing Prokoviev all day and there is nothing I would like better than to play something straightforward and simple.'

We came to the first carol and I began to strum but then suddenly Harry began to play and the whole audience seemed to warm and smile in astonishment. They were hearing a virtuoso! Gripped by the pure beauty of the sound, they began to sing. It was quite an experience. All I could do was plonk away but this enormously talented helper turned the whole thing into something wonderful.

And that is a picture of the work of the great Helper, the Holy Spirit. Sometimes we as pastors look at ourselves, our inadequate sermon notes and our other efforts for the church and feel just how inept and unworthy we are. But we are not alone. As we ask God, the Holy Spirit will come, stand with us and turn our meagre efforts into something unexpectedly beautiful and powerful to the glory of God. The Holy Spirit is your friend in the study, in the pulpit, and out on the road visiting and counselling.

So these verses give us hope. They begin to build our resilience. Sincere Timothy is reminded of God's capability as he focuses on the profound priority of gospel ministry.

Exercise for those in ministry

This chapter saw the apostle Paul beginning to act as a friend and father to Timothy and give advice and exhortation regarding his troubles and his ministry.

- Make a list of three people who are close to you who would be both qualified and willing to fulfil this role for you. They must be mature Christians to whom you look as role models. If you are able to list more than one such person, think through their different gifts and the areas in which they have experience with regard to pastoral life.
- What kind of problems would it be best to refer to which one?
- If you are married, ministry must work for both you and your wife. Is there someone she is able to look to as a friend and a mother as a ministry wife? Talk and pray this through together.

3

Strength from God's Grace

*You know that everyone in the province of Asia has deserted me,
including Phygelus and Hermogenes.*

*May the Lord show mercy to the household of Onesiphorus,
because he often refreshed me and was not ashamed of my chains.
On the contrary, when he was in Rome, he searched hard for me
until he found me. May the Lord grant that he will find mercy
from the Lord on that day! You know very well in how many ways
he helped me in Ephesus.*

*You then, my son, be strong in the grace that is in Christ Jesus.
And the things you have heard me say in the presence of many
witnesses entrust to reliable men who will also be qualified to teach
others. (2 Tim. 1:15–2:2)*

I have had to change some of the details for reasons of
confidentiality and security, but this is a true story.

There had been a road accident and the young
missionary woman, Phoebe, on the field less than two
years, had ended up in a rural prison in Asia. The only
Westerner in the women's wing, sharing a cell with three

or four local women, she was far from home, cut off from Christian fellowship and terribly alone. Sometimes our resilience for Christ is put to the test in major ways.

An older colleague, Veronica, found where she was and began regular visits. Veronica brought encouragement through kindness, God's Word and prayer. And it made all the difference, strengthening the younger woman amid her time of trial. She didn't go to pieces; she proved resilient.

Veronica knew the power of humour (Prov. 17:22), and one thing she did was to give her young friend a tiny rubber duck that quacked when you squeezed it. It raised a smile. When Phoebe got back to the cell, the local women frowned and looked quizzically at the duck. Then Phoebe made it quack and they all fell about laughing. Could they each have one?

On a subsequent visit, Veronica obliged. The women were delighted. It led to a greater friendliness.

Not long after that, Veronica was visiting the prison once again to see Phoebe. As she approached, the armed guard looked at her very sternly. What was the matter? Veronica carried on walking, looked down and didn't meet his eyes. Then, just as she was passing him suddenly she heard 'quack, quack'. She looked around. There was the guard with a big smile on his face with one of the rubber ducks! They both giggled.

Veronica's visits had not only strengthened Phoebe spiritually, she had brought a new atmosphere to that grim prison. (By the way the story has a happy ending— not too long after, everything was sorted out and Phoebe released.)

I don't think that Onesiphorus took a rubber duck to Paul's jail when he met up with him! But his visit certainly refreshed Paul (1:16) and encouraged him as the apostle was in prison in Rome. The prison system of Caesar's empire was not like ours. Paul may have been held in a private home or a cell owned commercially in a backstreet rather than a public prison. That is why it took time for Onesiphorus to find him (1:17). But it helped Paul greatly to know he wasn't forgotten and that this man was not ashamed of him and took trouble to find him.

A supportive network?

We need resilience as Christian workers, and one of the key factors we can identify which brings strength and helps us to be resilient is strong relationships and a supportive social network. This is one of the blessings of a good church fellowship. We support one another. We stand together. There are so many 'one another' commands in the New Testament. We are to love one another, honour one another, be kind and compassionate to one another, and much more. And that work of 'one anothering' can contribute gigantically to our resilience.

But having said that, of course, we have to be realistic enough to accept that sometimes other people can be a terrible source of discouragement too. Those who had once followed Paul in the province of Asia had now turned away from him (1:15). It seems that it was the faithlessness and desertion of others which made the faithful friendship of Onesiphorus stand out in Paul's mind. It reminds us that though it is good to draw strength from other Christians and be refreshed by them we must not look to them too much. Perhaps it is with this in mind that Paul gives his great command to Timothy to find strength in God and His grace as he begins to write what we call chapter 2: 'You then, my son, be strong in the grace that is in Christ Jesus.' Look to Christ first of all, not to others.

God has grace for Timothy and grace for us too. So it will be helpful for us to linger over verse 1 and examine three dimensions of God's grace in Christ Jesus. Don't miss this. **Strength, courage and resilience for difficult times are found in God's grace.** Resilience is not first of all gained by more commitment or determination on our part. Peter's protestations that, though everyone else might deny Jesus, he would not, exemplify this. He was sincere but it got him nowhere. The necessary zeal, energy and grit to keep going in ministry cannot be summoned up from within us—or if they are, they are likely to lead us into burn-out.

Rather, strength is found in God and particularly in taking hold of God's grace by faith. The good news is that God has grace for all needy Christians, but here we are reminded especially for Christian leaders like Timothy who feel their failure and frailty.

We have already asked the question, 'What is grace?' We answered by saying, 'It is God's lovingly favourable attitude towards us in Christ.' But now let's unpack that further, particularly using the context of 2 Timothy chapter 1. Retracing our steps we recognise three ways in which God's grace helps the faltering pastor.

Grace for salvation

Paul has directed Timothy to God's grace: 'You then, my son, be strong in the grace that is in Christ Jesus' (2:1).

Salvation is where we must always begin. But nothing undermines our joy, confidence and courage like salvation by works. We imagine our standing with God depends on how well we are doing as a Christian, or even as a pastor, and of course we can never be sure we've done enough. Instead of our faith being in Christ alone, it is at least partially in our own efforts. Once we examine them, we always find they fall short of what could have been done and certainly fail the infinitely perceptive test of God's holy eyes. So, looking to our deeds, we must conclude that we are not sure at all that God loves us (why should He?) and is with us. That's when we crumble.

But what did Paul say in chapter 1? 'God...has saved us and called us to a holy life—not because of anything we have done but because of his own purpose and grace.' (1:9) It's not by works in any way. It is by grace. That grace was given not earned. Notice 'given'. It was a free gift. Notice also: 'This grace was given us in Christ Jesus before the beginning of time' (1:9), so it does not and cannot depend on us. *First,* Christ is the means or medium for the imparting of grace—not us or our works. *Second,* the decision that we should be recipients of grace took place long before we were ever born. And now this grace for us, planned in eternity past, has been revealed in Christ (1:10), so that life and immortality for sinners has been brought to light through the manifestation of Jesus raised from the dead. Christ has done it all. And if Christ has done it all, then despite all our many failings we can be confident.

It should not be so, but pastors especially often need reminding that salvation is not by works. However, we forget grace for many reasons.

Sometimes it is due to an imbalanced preaching of holiness, which forgets the fact that the New Testament always teaches the imperative of sanctification in the context of the indicative of what God has already done for us through Christ in grace.[1] When we forget, we feel it's all down to us.

Sometimes a pastor feels so under pressure with people and problems and with so little help that he foolishly tries to take comfort in some sin. Then his conscience roars at him, 'How can God possibly put up with you?' He feels he must do some kind of 'penance' because he is a pastor and not just an ordinary sinner to make up for his failure. He has forgotten Christ and grace.

Sometimes it is because the church the pastor is serving wants 'value for money' and so a conscientious pastor begins to neglect unseen time with God to be refreshed by grace and concentrate on ministry that is seen—so that he is seen not to be slacking. 'It's works that count' is the message the pastor has unconsciously imbibed and he topples over into a legalistic mentality, which destroys any honest man's confidence. We need to listen again to the gospel of grace. Listen to Martin Luther:

> A Christian is both righteous and a sinner, an enemy of God yet a child of God. These contraries no sophister will admit for they know not the manner of justification. But we teach and comfort the afflicted sinner in this

---

1. See Sinclair Ferguson, *Devoted to God* (Banner of Truth, 2016).

manner: 'Brother it is not possible for thee to become so righteous in this life that thou should feel no sin at all…'

But thou wilt say: 'How can I be holy when I feel sin in me?' I answer in that thou dost feel and acknowledge thy sin, it is a good token: give thanks to God and despair not. It is one step to health when the sick man acknowledges his infirmity. 'But how shall I be delivered from sin?' Run to Christ, the physician that healeth them that are broken in heart, and saveth sinners. If thou believe thou art righteous for thou giveth glory unto God…and that sin that remaineth in thee is not laid to thy charge, but is pardoned for Christ's sake in whom thou believest, who is perfectly just: whose righteousness is your righteousness, and thy sin took upon himself.[2]

There is grace for the pastor's failures and the pastor's sins—grace for salvation.

Grace for significance

How shall we pastors find strength when we lead just a small church perhaps despised by the world? We feel so insignificant. We feel at times as if we might be wasting our lives. How can we carry on?

The answer is not to accept the world's estimation of your significance but understand whom God has made you by grace. Clues to the Christian's true significance are scattered all over the opening verses of 2 Timothy chapter 1.

---

2. Martin Luther, *Commentary on Galatians* (3:6) (Kregel Publications, 1979), page 130.

Look again at 2:1: 'You then, my son, be strong in the grace that is in Christ Jesus.' Why is Timothy Paul's son? It is because he has been born again through the word of the gospel Paul preached and so has become God's son too! Look again at that verse. We find grace in Christ Jesus because the Christian is in Christ Jesus. We are united to Him! That woman just looks like anyone else, nothing special. Yes, but do you know who she is married to—who she is united to—who her husband is? Jesus Christ—the Lord of the universe. Forget the US President's wife. *She* truly is the first lady! You can apply that to yourself as an individual Christian (Rom. 7:3-4) or, pastor, to that little church you serve, which is the bride of Christ.

Look at 1:14: 'Guard the good deposit that was entrusted to you—guard it with the help of the Holy Spirit who lives in us.' The Holy Spirit, the personal power of God through whom all creation sprung into being, dwells in us. Furthermore, to us has been entrusted the good deposit of the gospel—the antidote to all the world's sicknesses and sins. What could be more significant than that?

Look at 1:9-10: 'This grace was given us in Christ Jesus... who has destroyed death and has brought life and immortality to light through the gospel.' That undistinguished man over there—do you know who he is? He is the heir to an untold fortune. Christian, you are an heir of God, a joint-heir with Jesus who inherits life and immortality and glory! Significance is written all over you as a Christian and as a pastor. The world in its blindness didn't see who Jesus was, so don't be surprised that they don't recognise who you are (1 John 3:1). But by God's grace, we can hold our heads up! That tin tabernacle in which your church meets and you teach God's Word is actually the most significant building in your town.

So fix your eyes on the grace of God and through faith in Christ draw strength from it.

Grace for suffering

Paul will say more about this in chapter 3 of his letter, but the last days in which we live will often provide an environment which is very antagonistic towards Christ, the gospel and our ministry. We will suffer. Paul has already put his cards on the table for Timothy: 'So do not be ashamed to testify about our Lord, or ashamed of me his prisoner. But join with me in suffering for the gospel by the power of God.' (1:8) Paul himself is facing death. How shall we find courage to suffer? We go back to our 2:1: 'You then, my son, be strong in the grace that is in Christ Jesus.' When the time comes for us to face suffering there will be grace for us to give us strength.

A part of Phoebe's story that I quoted at the beginning of the chapter comes in at this point. She was a young missionary and very new to the field. But she would tell Veronica when she visited, something like this: 'Do thank all the people who are praying for me. But this is not as hard as you might think. God has been richly blessing my soul in this prison. I wouldn't be anywhere else!' God will provide grace for us in our time of need as we suffer.

And the New Testament gives us many reasons to rejoice in suffering for Christ. Here are three which might help us.

- First, let's remind ourselves again that God brings about His gracious plans through our suffering. That's one of the reasons Paul invites Timothy to join him in suffering for the gospel (1:8). It's because it furthers the gospel. That's why Paul could write to the Corinthians: 'Death is at work in us, but life is at work in you.' (2 Cor. 4:12) That's why Elijah was disappointed at Mount Carmel. He wanted God's kingdom to come by dramatic power. He thought the fire from heaven and the sonic 'boom!' would do it. But the nation of Israel was not turned. During the sequel on Mount Horeb, God underlines the lesson. There was great wind and fire and earthquake. But God was in none of them. Rather, he was in the still small voice (1 Kings 19:11-12). That is why Elijah does not come at the cross when the onlookers hope for his appearance (Matt. 27:49). It is because the kingdom comes by sacrifice, not a spectacular show. When we understand that our suffering is not in vain but will prosper the kingdom, we find strength, courage and resilience to suffer.

- Second, of course, our suffering for Christ leads to glory. It actually even increases the glory awaiting us. Paul speaks ironically but truly when he says: 'For our light and momentary troubles are achieving for us an eternal glory that far outweighs them all.' (2 Cor. 4:17) When we can see suffering in that positive way, we are given new resilience.

- Third, our suffering can open up new avenues of service for Christ. A dear friend, Nancy—now with the Lord—suffered Méniere's disease. This is a disease of the inner ear, which brings dizziness and sickness and deafness. But instead of feeling sorry for herself, Nancy decided that she would use her disability to reach out to the new community God had placed her in—people who were deaf! Like Paul in prison reaching out to his guards (Phil. 1:12-13), she would often open her home to deaf folk and provide celebrations and parties with the gospel, especially at Christmas and Easter. Not only was she given grace to endure her suffering, but she used her suffering to forward the gospel.

How can we find resilience? The key verse is 2:1: 'You then, my son, be strong in the grace that is in Christ Jesus.' And having reminded Timothy of where to find strength, Paul goes straight on again to underline the job with which he wants Timothy to get on.

Training others

Prompted by the prevalence of false teaching and so many leaving the faith, Paul is concerned to tell Timothy to get on with getting the truth out there: 'And the things you have heard me say in the presence of many witnesses entrust to reliable men who will also be qualified to teach others.' (2:2) This strategy of training up others in the truths of the gospel is part and parcel of Paul's concern that the gospel be kept and guarded for the future (1:13-14). How is Timothy going to find the energy? Our key verse, verse 1, of course precedes verse 2. Here the command comes into play again: 'You then, my son, be strong in the grace that is in Christ Jesus.'

Earlier in the chapter, we noted that a good supportive network of friends can really help us to keep going as Christians and as Christian ministers. Perhaps Paul knew that if Timothy could meet with others and pass on the things which he had learned from the apostle Paul to others, then a band of brothers might just grow around Timothy. Not only would the main matter of guarding the gospel be advanced, but perhaps also a group of mutually supportive friends in the gospel might well emerge. It is the gospel itself which not only encourages us as individuals but also draws us into fellowship with one another. Nothing has the power to produce real depth of fellowship like the gospel. Seeing the love of God, we are led to love one another.

If what I am suggesting is right here, then it might explain the problem with many pastors' 'fraternals'. I can remember talking to a friend in the ministry about why he did not attend his local pastors' group. 'I used to go,' he said, 'but I always seemed to come away discouraged. So I stopped going. It wasn't doing me any good.'

I think his experience is actually quite common. But I would suggest that the reason so many fraternals, though full of good intentions, actually fail is because they concentrate on the wrong things. So often the fraternal focuses on the churches and the pastors—their ups and downs. If one church is down, it tends to depress everyone. If one church is up and others are not, then the others feel jealous and disappointed with their lot. Instead of focusing on ourselves, fraternals need to learn to focus again on Christ and the gospel—the things Timothy heard the apostle Paul say in the presence of many witnesses (2:2). This will both encourage and build fellowship. Get that right first and then the fraternal will be in a far better position to handle the ups and downs.

Coffee on the wall—'Be strong in the grace that is in Christ Jesus'

I have a Chinese friend who loves to send me stories which warm his heart. He sent this tale to me and I often come back to it to remind myself of the freeness of grace.

> I sat with a friend in a well-known coffee shop in a town near Venice, the city of lights and water. As we enjoyed our coffee, a man entered and sat at an empty table. He called the waiter, placing his order saying, 'Two cups of coffee, one on the wall.' We heard these words with interest and observed he was served a cup of coffee but paid for two. When he left, the waiter stuck a piece of paper on the wall saying, 'A cup of coffee'. While we were still there, two other men entered and ordered 3 cups of coffee, '2 on the table 1 on the wall'. They paid for 3 cups and left, and another piece of paper went up on the wall. It was something unique and intriguing for us. We eventually left.
>
> After a few days of sight-seeing we had a chance to go to this coffee shop again. While we were there this time a very poorly dressed man entered. As he seated himself, he looked at the wall and said to the waiter, 'One cup of coffee from the wall.' The waiter served coffee just as for others. The man drank it and left with no charge. We were amazed to watch all this, as the waiter took off a piece of paper from the wall and threw it in the bin.

Now it was no mystery to us—the matter was very clear. The great care and respect shown by the inhabitants of this town to the poor brought tears to our eyes.

The story is a picture of grace, favour and free kindness to the poor and needy, no matter who they are or how undeserving they might be. Sometimes, we as Christian leaders can be very aware of just how spiritually poor and underserving we are. But there is grace for us. Christ has paid. He has put it on the wall for us. 'You then, my son, be strong in the grace that is in Christ Jesus.'

Exercise for those in ministry

Thankfully, resilience in ministry is not primarily about gritting our teeth, putting on a stiff upper lip and holding back the tears. We have been reminded in this chapter that God has grace for flawed and failing pastors.

The three different areas highlighted in this chapter for which we were reminded that God has grace are for our sins, for our significance and for our suffering.

What are your own besetting sins? What makes you feel that your job in ministry is to no purpose? What do you most fear with regard to suffering? Write out an inventory for yourself in these three areas and bring them to God in prayer.

Spend half an hour finding promises in Scripture of God's grace for sinners, sufferers and nobodies. Write out the texts you find. Ask God to make you confident in what He has promised.

4

Mindset for Resilience

Endure hardship with us like a good soldier of Christ Jesus. No one serving as a soldier gets involved in civilian affairs – he wants to please his commanding officer. Similarly, if anyone competes as an athlete, he does not receive the victor's crown unless he competes according to the rules. The hardworking farmer should be the first to receive a share of the crops. Reflect on what I am saying, for the Lord will give you insight into all this.

Remember Jesus Christ, raised from the dead, descended from David. This is my gospel, for which I am suffering even to the point of being chained like a criminal. But God's word is not chained. Therefore I endure everything for the sake of the elect, that they too may obtain the salvation that is in Christ Jesus, with eternal glory.

Here is a trustworthy saying: If we died with him, we will also live with him; if we endure, we will also reign with him. If we disown him, he will also disown us; if we are faithless, he will remain faithful, for he cannot disown himself. (2 Tim. 2:3-13)

———————

The name Martin Withers may not be familiar to you. Let me explain who he is and what he and his friends did.

In early April 1982, Argentina invaded the remote UK colony of the Falkland Islands just off the South American coast in the South Atlantic. It was thought that the British would not have the political will or determination to reclaim them, given their relative insignificance and the huge distance, 8,000 miles, from London. But the Argentinian *Junta*, headed by General Galtieri, had badly miscalculated. A naval task force and troops were sent from the UK.

There was an airport on the islands which was crucial. If the Argentinians could use it, unimpeded, to fly in supplies and to base their Mirage fighter jets there, it would make the job of taking back the colony much more difficult. The runway at Port Stanley airfield needed to be attacked and, if possible, made unusable. No planes from the task force's aircraft carriers *Hermes* and *Invincible* were able to deliver a sufficiently heavy payload to make the required impact. And so it was that a plan was developed for the RAF to utilise its ageing Vulcan bombers, carrying twenty-one 1,000lb bombs, in what became known as operation *Black Buck*.

In many ways, it was a crazy scheme. The Vulcans would fly from Ascension Island off the coast of West Africa to the Falklands, a distance of 4,000 miles, using in-flight refuelling from a series of Victor tankers, which had not only to service the bombers, but also refuel one another in a complicated relay operation. The first raid was to use two Vulcans, one to deliver the bombs and one as the back-up. Martin Withers was the pilot of the back-up Vulcan.

From the very outset of the raid, problems arose. The prime bomber developed a fault and had to turn back. It was now down to Withers and his crew. Then, one of the in-flight refuelling planes had to drop out too. As the long flight proceeded, it became clear that the instrumentation in the antiquated Vulcan was unreliable. Navigation presented huge problems. Still they pressed on. It would take around eight hours flying time to get there. As they eventually neared the Falklands, the weather deteriorated and there was an electrical storm. Then the realisation hit that the refuelling schedule was going to pot. Their estimates concerning how much fuel was needed were way out. The Vulcan was left with insufficient fuel to complete the attack and then rendezvous with the next tanker.

It was at this point that Martin Withers asked his crew whether they should pursue their mission or abort. With limited fuel, they knew that to complete the operation could mean having to ditch the aircraft and come down in the cold waters of the South Atlantic. He was up for it. However, not only his own life, but the lives of his men were at stake. So he put the question to them.

One by one, and in quick succession, the answers came back from his crew members through the intercom: 'Well, we've come this far…'; 'Keep going'; 'Got to go on with the mission.' So at great risk, Vulcan 607 would press home the attack.[1]

That takes guts and endurance, bravery and resilience. With so much at stake and the odds stacked against them, it would have been easy to turn back. But they didn't. They

---

1. Rowland White, *Vulcan 607* (Bantam Press, 2006).

persevered. They had a job to do and they were going to do it whatever it took.

Churches need pastors with something of that kind of backbone and grit. So we ask, 'Where does such a determined mindset come from? And how is it cultivated?' That is what we investigate in this chapter. Pastors are not bomber pilots. Nor are they aircrew. But we are involved in a deadly spiritual warfare in which we crave victory for the kingdom of God and the name of Jesus. We are charged with a task of fighting to take back territory that has been captured by God's enemy—the precious, eternal souls of lost men and women.

Three times in this section of his letter Paul refers to 'endurance'. He wants Timothy not to drop out but to push on. He challenges Timothy to endure suffering (2:3). He speaks about his own willingness to endure (2:10). Using what seems to be a well-known saying among early Christians, he reminds us that endurance is necessary in every true Christian's life (2:12). How does Paul go about encouraging Timothy to endure and to be resilient?

Seeing ourselves

One of the most important factors is a biblical self-image. The way we think of ourselves and what we are doing crucially affects our attitudes and therefore our resilience. For instance, take the simple example of a downpour of rain hitting an English village in May. A cricketer who was looking forward to playing a match on the green will be very put out and may fall into self-pity. 'Why does it always rain when I have the chance to open the batting?' A sour mood may well follow. He's a cricketer. But the local farmer, who needs water for his crops, will see things very differently. He could not be happier to see the rain. The cricketer sees it one way, the farmer another. Their 'identities' influence their reactions.

Similarly, if pastors see themselves the way the world caricatures us—inept fools involved in a no-hope, out-of-date project that is bound for failure—we are likely to struggle and will not keep going long in the work when the pressure is on. But if we see ourselves as we really are in Christ, God's children, summoned to a vital work by our Father and with ultimate victory guaranteed, we are likely to show far more resilience. It is a matter of mindset.

In order to instil a resilient outlook into Timothy, Paul provides his young partner with three graphics (ways of seeing himself), three guarantees and a reality check.

Paul gives Timothy three graphics (2:3-7)

As we have noted already, Timothy suffers frequent illness; he is naturally somewhat timid; his youth and inexperience easily lead him to feel useless; churches are being misled and ravaged by false teaching; congregations are down because people are deserting the faith; Paul himself is about to die and there is persecution from people who are very nasty pieces of work. No wonder Timothy seems on the point of giving up as a church leader. It cannot be denied that his situation is rough.

But the way Timothy reacts will depend on how he sees himself. So Paul draws three portraits, three pictures for Timothy to think on and chew over (2:7) with the Lord's help. Timothy needs to see himself as a soldier (2:3), an athlete (2:5) and a farmer (2:6).

We are soldiers

'Endure hardship with us like a good soldier of Christ Jesus. No one serving as a soldier gets involved in civilian affairs—he wants to please his commanding officer.' (2:3-4) Martin Withers and his crew were in the forces. Paul wants us to have something of their outlook. Let's just take three points about soldiering.

First, when we signed up to the ministry, we signed up for hardship and sacrifice. That's what soldiering involves. It is not peacetime for God's kingdom. We are at war. In fact, the suffering side of soldiering is not just true of pastors but of every authentic Christian. Jesus said: 'If anyone would come after me, he must deny himself and take up his cross and follow me. For whoever wants to save his life will lose it, but whoever loses his life for me and for the gospel will save it.' (Mark 8:34-35) But taking seriously the words of Jesus helps us to see the required suffering and sacrifice in a totally different way. We are in the process of saving our lives, not losing them. When trouble hits and ministry is painful, we can tell ourselves on Christ's own authority, 'I'm saving my life.' When we feel we have lost all the chances in life that our contemporaries have taken and capitalized on, let the words of Jesus sink in: 'Whoever loses his life for me and the gospel will save it.'

Second, Paul reminds us here of a concept which is out of fashion in the church ('so last year') but which is biblical. It is the concept of duty. A duty is a moral or legal obligation. Soldiers who sign up for the forces are legally obligated to do their duty. We are morally obligated to Christ Jesus, who loves us and died to rescue us from eternal damnation, to do our duty for Him. Jesus Himself tells us that His servants have a duty to Him. When we do what Jesus commands us, we have only done our duty (Luke 17:10). Soldiers are not there to please themselves but to do their duty—that is to carry out the orders of their commanding officer. A soldier who does his duty, no matter what the opposition or how scared he might be feeling, is a good soldier. Paul calls Timothy to be a good soldier of Christ Jesus. He calls us too.

Third, what is the incentive? It is not only the smile of our commander, Jesus Christ, but it is the prospect of victory. As we battle for Christ, we shall inherit eternal life and eternal rewards. Imagine being one of the soldiers in Gideon's army as they face the hosts of Midian. An offer is sent out to every man that if they are not up for the fight they are free to go home (Judges 7:3-4). Many departed. But I bet so many of those men who walked away kicked themselves later. Gideon routed the Midianites in that daring battle. They had the chance to make history, they had the opportunity to be heroes, they could have been able to say, 'I was there that night when we broke our empty jars, let our torches flare, sounded our trumpets and saw the enemy go to pieces.' But they turned the chance down. They bottled it. 'Timothy, don't let that happen to you by ducking out of the fight!' Don't let it happen to us. Be a good soldier.

We are athletes

'Similarly, if anyone competes as an athlete, he does not receive the victor's crown unless he competes according to the rules.' (2:5)

73

If the key concept for the soldier is duty, then for the athlete it is discipline. When things are difficult, when the competition is ferocious, when the world is watching, the temptation is to cut corners, to cheat. In recent years, the sport of cycling has been dogged by scandals over performance-enhancing drugs. Those who were thought to be great champions have been stripped of their medals and written out of the record books. In athletics, the whole team of Russian Olympians was banned from competition because of evidence of state-sponsored use of illegal substances. Athletes must do things right or be disqualified. It was the same in Paul's day.

There were many false teachers contemporary with Timothy who were changing the gospel in order to make it more palatable and more attractive. They were drawing many people away after them. Indeed, there are rewards in heaven for those who turn many to Christ and to righteousness (Dan. 12:3). But think of the eternal ignominy of those who have built large churches only for it to be exposed on Judgment Day that their ministry had been an utter fraud. They had actually not kept the rules. They had preached themselves, not Christ Jesus as Lord. They had preached another Christ, who is no Christ at all.

There is a crown to be won. But Paul is reminding Timothy that it must be won legitimately. That requires discipline. It means sticking to the true way. It means keeping going. See yourself as an athlete. Tell yourself during the uphill periods, 'Discipline will lead to that crown. Indiscipline will not.' Tell yourself, 'Adopt the athlete's mindset.'

We are farmers

'The hardworking farmer should be the first to receive a share of the crops.' (2:6)

I talked some time ago to another Christian leader who ministers to ministers and often counsels pastors in difficulty. His observation was that often pastors face a crisis at around forty-five years old. The back story he discerns is something like this. By the time they are forty-five, they have usually been in the ministry around ten years or more. Ten years in they are often on their second church. The first church had its problems, some people gave the pastor a hard time. Among other things, he faced the fiery darts of stroppy unexplained letters of resignation from the church designed to hurt. And so it was that he and his family moved on to the second church. But after a few years, it begins to dawn that this church is basically the same. And so the crisis comes. 'What are we doing with our lives?' Ministry is painful, often backbreaking work. It's a slog and it always will be wherever you go. And harvests aren't instant, especially spiritual ones. But that's how it is for farmers. To have an expectation of an instant crop is unrealistic and will only lead to disappointment. But there will be a harvest. It simply takes time.

Though like the athlete, the farmer is focused on one thing, in this case growing crops, nevertheless agricultural work has many aspects to it. The key idea here is diligence. He has to pay continual attention to a variety of things. If the farmer pursues his tasks of ploughing and planting and watering and covering the young plants on the frosty nights, and continuing to clear the weeds and spreading fertilizer and keeping off the parasites and much more—

it will happen. The harvest will emerge—guaranteed. Yes, the weather is crucial and that's in God's hands. But even with the very worst of summers, it is unheard of for there to be no harvest whatsoever. A harvest will come. The size is down to the Lord. But it will come, if the farmer is diligent.

He must not give up too soon. If the farmer plants in February, the wheat will not be ready until August. It's no good giving up at the end of May because the harvest has not yet come. And frequently pastors move on to that second or third church in May. If they had only waited and ridden out the storms they would have reaped a harvest. They would have experienced the joy of knowing they had been used by God. They would have been able humbly to get on their knees with an overflowing heart before the Lord and celebrate that on such days, the ministry is the best work in the world! The pastor would have seen God's blessing and the church pull together around him as they realised that God has and does use him. He would have had a share of God's crop.

Perhaps one of the greatest challenges wrapped up in this picture of a farmer as we reflect on it, is that farmers tend to be anonymous people. No one knows who it was who grew the wheat for that loaf of bread they are now enjoying. No one knows who tended the orchard where that scrumptious apple was on a tree. But the prospect of the promised harvest at God's time should enable us to embrace the obscurity and to diligently keep at the work.

The soldier does his duty. The athlete keeps his discipline. The farmer works with diligence. A mindset, inspired by grace, of duty plus discipline plus diligence equals resilience.

It is worth noting that the outlook of these three was a major part of Paul's own thinking about his ministry. It is the first two metaphors which obviously underlie his famous summary of his ministry towards the end of the letter: 'I have fought the good fight, I have finished the race, I have kept the faith. Now there is in store for me the crown of righteousness…' (2 Tim. 4:7) It is the picture of the athlete which is in Paul's mind as he addresses the Ephesian elders for the last time: 'I consider my life worth nothing to me, if only I may finish the race and complete the task the Lord has given me—the task of testifying to the gospel of God's grace.' (Acts 20:24) It is the picture of the hardworking farmer which is in view as he writes to the Corinthians: 'I planted the seed, Apollos watered it, but God made it grow.' (1 Cor. 3:6) Pastor, you need to get into this way of thinking about yourself.

Paul gives Timothy three guarantees (2:8-10)

I listened to the story of a pastor not long ago who had been in the middle of two years' blessing in his church but simultaneously agonised over whether he himself was actually saved. Thankfully, it was later resolved. But it shows that even leaders can have grave doubts.

We can imagine troubled Timothy saying to himself, 'Yes Paul, it's all very well saying I need the mindset of a soldier and an athlete and a farmer, but how do we know there will be a crown, a crop and a commendation from our commanding officer?' With such a question in mind, Paul now comes in with three guarantees. He points

Timothy to three plain facts which show that the work of the ministry is worthwhile and will be well rewarded. He tells Timothy to remember God's Christ, God's Word and God's elect.

God's Christ

'Remember Jesus Christ, raised from the dead, descended from David. This is my gospel.' (2:8)

We can get too used to that word 'gospel'. Let's just translate it as 'good news' for a moment. Paul speaks of 'my good news'. It is his, personally. It is not simply his, in that he preaches it. It is not simply his, because God entrusted it to him. It is his, in that it is the joy of his own heart, the tremendous set of facts he knows to be true and keeps him going in life. It is the news which sets his soul on fire and that he can't wait to tell others.

In particular, it is Paul's good news which saved him from a life of bitter, religious bigotry and from a lost eternity. And he knows it's true because he saw and heard and met and was spoken to personally by the once dead, but now alive, Lord Jesus. He is as sure about this good news as about anything that a human being can know through their five senses—as sure about it as the solidity of the Damascus Road under his feet, or as that he would know his own mother if he saw her.

Jesus Christ being alive from the dead means that Christianity is true and, therefore, all other religions and ideologies are ultimately false. And that means that any way of spending your life other than being a Christian is worse than a waste of time.

There are three nuances in the way Paul phrases his words here worth noting.

Immediacy: Though the historical fact of Jesus' resurrection is obviously conveyed, yet it is not what is mainly in mind. Donald Guthrie comments on this verse: 'The passive participle "raised from the dead" draws attention to a present experience of the risen Lord, which would be particularly underlined by Paul's own conversion.'[2] In other words, though the resurrection is a fact of history, it also means that the living Christ is a fact of personal experience. It means He is with us. It means we are not on our own in the ministry.

Continuity: In his Epistles Paul links the resurrection of Jesus to His being descended from David only here and in the opening verses of Romans. There, Paul was addressing a church in which there were frictions between Jews and Gentiles though the gospel is for both. At times, preaching the gospel stirred much opposition from some Jews both for Paul and Timothy. But actually the gospel honours Jewish history. Around 1000 B.C. God promised David a descendant who would rule the nations forever. That was no empty promise. Christ's resurrection shows God is faithful. The Christian ministry is therefore guaranteed worthwhile.

Sovereignty: Paul's words here are redolent with royalty. Christ is God's anointed King. He is descended from the greatest king of Israel. But David, who brought victory, prosperity and peace to God's people, was just

---

2. Donald Guthrie, *The Pastoral Epistles*, Tyndale NT Commentaries (Tyndale Press, 1957), page 143.

a picture of the marvellous reality of Jesus, whose benign sovereignty brings eternal protection, peace and prosperity to all His people.

Timothy is to remember these things and not let them slip. Have we let them slip? Is that why the devil has got the advantage over us?

God's Word

'This is my gospel, for which I am suffering even to the point of being chained like a criminal. But God's word is not chained.' (2:8-9)

Paul is suffering. It is to be expected. He and other preachers are bringing good news for broken and needy sinners. But, for the world system of Satan's kingdom and those who prosper and are in positions of authority under that system, we bring news of another King, who is bent on overthrowing their self-serving and exploitative racket.

Jesus has come to turn the world upside down, to bring down rulers from their thrones and lift up the humble. Of course, there is going to be a backlash from them. Satan will use everything he can to shut up a preacher. Paul was under lock and key from the authorities. The devil might have other ways of trying his best to shut us up.

But God's Word cannot be thwarted (2:8-9). It will spread. It will not return to God without achieving its purpose (Isa. 55:11). It cannot be contained.

We are given a number of striking evidences of this in Acts. The apostles are locked in prison in Jerusalem, but angels come to set them free (Acts 5:19; 12:5-7) and so the Word of God continued to spread (Acts 12:24). Paul and Silas are imprisoned in Philippi for the gospel, but the great earthquake at midnight shakes off the chains and wrecks the prison doors and the jailer himself and his family become Christians (Acts 16:32-33). By the time he is in prison in Rome, Paul knows that he doesn't even have to be released from his chains for the gospel to spread. His time locked up had led to the gospel spreading among the palace guard and had encouraged other Christians to be bolder in sharing their faith (Phil. 1:12-14).

God's Word cannot be chained. And we pastors and preachers have the privilege of being vehicles in the proclamation of that unstoppable Word. It is a living Word. It is guaranteed to spread.

I am reminded of a story from The Gideons organisation from a few years ago. A hotel in one of the more expensive resorts in Brazil (I think) had decided it was time to dispense with the Bibles in each room, in the bedside tables. It was a thing of the past, the management thought, and not for the modern world. So the Bibles ended up in a skip outside the hotel. But a passing workman picked up one of the Bibles. He began to read it. He came to Christ. And from there a church soon started with others being saved. God's Word cannot be stopped. So it is guaranteed that, as we are faithful expositors and communicators of the Bible, our ministries will be effective. Here is another stimulus to have the mindset of a good soldier doing his duty, a dedicated athlete pursuing his discipline, a hard-working farmer diligently going about his task.

God's elect

'Therefore I endure everything for the sake of the elect, that they too may obtain the salvation that is in Christ Jesus, with eternal glory.' (2:10)

Because Christ is alive and the word of God cannot be thwarted, God's eternal plans will come to pass. His chosen people, the elect, will be saved. And God has chosen us, as pastors and preachers, to be part of the means through which He achieves this certain goal. Therefore, says Paul, it is worth suffering and enduring hardship and being resilient. In Romans 8:30, Paul spells out the unbreakable chain of events which lead to salvation: 'And those he predestined, he also called; those he called, he also justified; those he justified he also glorified.'

Why is that last verb in the past tense? Why does it say 'glorified' instead of the future 'will be glorified' or the present tense (of those already in heaven) 'are being glorified'? The answer is because the destination of God's elect in glory is so certain that it might as well already have happened. This is an example of Paul's use of 'the prophetic past tense'.

But notice, we have a small part in that great chain of salvation. Those He predestined He called. God uses us, He uses our voices, He uses our preaching of the gospel to call those sinners to Himself. What an honour God has bestowed upon us as pastors and preachers. Therefore, let's have a resilient mindset.

We may see adverse times. We may see periods when there are no converts. Yet the fruit of our ministry is guaranteed. The elect, chosen by God, will be saved. So keep going.

Paul gives Timothy a reality check (2:11-13)

Here is a trustworthy saying:

> *If we died with him, we will also live with him;*
> *If we endure, we will also reign with him.*
> *If we disown him, he will also disown us;*
> *If we are faithless, he will remain faithful, for he cannot disown*
> *himself.*

This may well be a fragment of an early Christian hymn. Some Bible commentators believe that's what the 'trustworthy sayings' are which we find in Paul's pastoral Epistles. These verses are composed of two pairs of memorable sayings, which are bottom-line realities for everyone who professes to be a follower of Christ.

The *first* couplet in 2:11b-12a relates to those who remain true to Christ. If we truly follow Him, dying to the world's ways of sin and safety, putting Jesus first come what may, then we will live. If we push on with that and endure suffering on earth, we will reign with Christ in heaven, in glory.

The *second* saying in 2:12b-13 relates to those who seem to start as Christians, but fall away, and don't endure. This scenario is spelt out in the parable of the sower. Genuine Christians, the elect, are known by their perseverance. Temporary Christians are not Christians at all. Jesus Himself warned us: 'Whoever acknowledges me before men, I will also acknowledge him before my Father in heaven. But whoever disowns me before men, I will disown him before my Father in heaven.' (Matt. 10:32-33)

And Paul closes this 'trustworthy saying' by warning us that Christ will be faithful to that. His faithfulness means

He will carry out His threats as well as His promises. Jesus cannot disown Himself. You will not find Him on Judgment Day saying, 'Oh no. It wasn't me who said that, it was someone else.'

Oh my! But that's the reality check Timothy needs to hear as he contemplates walking out of the ministry and perhaps on Christ.

In our culture, where everything has to be positive, we may not be used to Paul's blunt and stern warning. But sometimes we need to be shown the shocking bottom line if we are going to have a resilient mindset in the Christian life and the Christian ministry.

Worthwhile?

Let me return briefly to Martin Withers and his comrades, whose story began this chapter. The crew of Vulcan 607 had the determination to press on to bomb the airstrip at Port Stanley, despite great danger. In fact, with some anticipation of their situation on the part of the refuelling crews they did get home safely. But not knowing that they would, the crew pressed home the attack. They didn't totally destroy the runway but they did manage to put a big crater in it.

This, of course, was quickly filled in by the Argentinian forces. Did this mean that their mission was a failure? Not at all. What the raid and subsequent raids showed was that, not only was the landing strip vulnerable, but also that the Argentinian mainland was within range of the Vulcans. This led to the Argentinians shifting their fighter jets to the mainland for protection, taking them out of the military equation and so making the retaking of the Falklands much easier.

Looking at the actual damage, so readily repaired, some critics doubted the value of operation *Black Buck*. But the psychological blow struck by the bombers leading to the withdrawal of the enemy fighters could be said to have been vital in regaining the Falklands.

It may be that cynics look at our preaching and pastoral ministry and conclude that its immediate effect is inconsequential. But just as the determined mindset of Withers and his crew in delivering their bombs made a huge difference in the long term, so persevering in delivering the Word of God is guaranteed to fulfil God's plans. Let's play our part and not give up.

Exercise for those in ministry

All Christians are called to put Christ first in their lives. We are to take seriously the fact that Jesus is Lord. Our duty to Him is to come before even our concern for ourselves (Mark 8:34, 35). This mindset underlies Paul's pictures of the Christian minister as a soldier, an athlete and a hardworking farmer.

In a phrase often used by a previous generation of Christians, we are to be crucified to self. To maintain such an attitude is an ongoing struggle for all Christians.

When was the last time you rededicated your life to Christ? Spend some time in prayer. Is now the time to surrender yourself again, as totally as you are able, to the will of the Lord Jesus Christ?

5
What should Resilience look like?

Keep reminding them of these things. Warn them before God against quarreling about words; it is of no value, and only ruins those who listen. Do your best to present yourself to God as one approved, a workman who does not need to be ashamed and who correctly handles the word of truth. Avoid godless chatter, because those who indulge in it will become more and more ungodly. Their teaching will spread like gangrene. Among them are Hymenaeus and Philetus, who have wandered away from the truth. They say that the resurrection has already taken place, and they destroy the faith of some. Nevertheless, God's solid foundation stands firm, sealed with this inscription: 'The Lord knows those who are his', and, 'Everyone who confesses the name of the Lord must turn away from wickedness.'

In a large house there are articles not only of gold and silver, but also of wood and clay; some for noble purposes and some for ignoble. If a man cleanses himself from the latter, he will be an instrument for noble purposes, made holy, useful to the Master and prepared to do any good work.

Flee the evil desires of youth, and pursue righteousness, faith, love and peace, along with all those who call on the Lord out of a pure heart. Don't have anything to do with foolish and stupid arguments, because they produce quarrels. And the Lord's servant must not quarrel; instead he must be kind to everyone, able to teach, not resentful. Those who oppose him he must gently instruct, in the hope that God will grant them repentance leading them to a knowledge of the truth, and that they will come to their senses and escape from the trap of the devil, who has taken them captive to do his will. (2 Tim. 2:14-26)

———————

What does resilience for Christ look like? You see, we can be resilient but not in a Christ-like way.

In the last chapter, we noted that Christian leaders need to have the mindset of a soldier combined with that of an athlete combined with that of a hardworking farmer. All those callings can be tough and it is not unknown for people who continually find that their lives are difficult and an uphill struggle to carry on but to become resentful of their hard path. They persevere but they become grim, obdurate and insensitive to others in the process. They can even become proud of their self-sacrifice and despise others.

Spurgeon tells a humorous story about a hard-headed Christian minister who had a reputation for being unwavering and unfeeling. This man was travelling on one of the steam trains of the time, and he put his head out of the carriage window to see ahead. The guard came along, recognised the man and saw him with his head out of the window. 'You must not put your head out,' said the guard. 'Why is that?' said the minister. 'There is some ironwork under one of the bridges we are approaching,' said the guard, 'and it might get damaged if your head struck it.' We can imagine the minister's indignation and the guard smiling to himself afterwards![1]

Thankfully, not all church leaders are like that—but some are. We need to be resilient, but resilience can easily turn into being inhuman, stubborn, bitter and unwilling to listen to others. Church leaders must be durable and determined without losing their kindness and joy.

Paul touches on this subject in this section. He says: 'The Lord's servant must not quarrel; instead he must be kind to everyone, able to teach, not resentful.' (2:24) Right in the middle of battling the devil's agents who oppose him (2:26), Timothy is to be kind and gentle. It's a Christ-like resilience that is required.

The verses we consider in this chapter give a wider angle on what true Christian resilience should be like, which is more than simply the need for the church leader to be loving. More than kindness is needed—but not less. Paul fills out the picture of what is required. We will note what he says under four headings.

Timothy is deeply discouraged. But there's a job to do. His work is teaching. Amidst the temptations and perils of the last days (3:1), churches need to be taught, guarded by truth or they will fall. That's the background. What does resilience in the context of a last-days ministry look like? If you are a church leader you need to know. Churches need to know too, so they can see what to look for in a leader and pray for their leaders.

---

1. C. H. Spurgeon, *Forgotten College Addresses*, ed. Terence Crosby (DayOne, 2016), page 20.

Resilience is to be characterised by seriousness, Scripture, sincerity and sympathy.

Genuine resilience is serious (2:14)

During World War Two many troops were transported to areas of conflict in the world on what had been luxury liners. My own father was disembarked into the disaster that was to become the fall of Singapore in 1942 from a cruise ship, which had been playing the schmaltzy 'I'll be with you in apple blossom time' over the Tannoy just before they docked. It turned into his introduction to ferocious conflict and three years' internment in the infamous Japanese POW camp of Changi Jail.

Churches can be warm places, like luxury cruise ships, and Christians can be so enamoured with comfort, they are taken by surprise by the battle. But the minister must never lose sight of the seriousness of the church's spiritual conflict and therefore of his task.

The church must be reminded

'Keep reminding them of these things.' (2:14a) Donald Guthrie comments: 'Men are to be put in remembrance of the things contained in the previously cited hymn or perhaps more generally of the teaching in the whole of the preceding part of the epistle.'

The 'trustworthy saying' in 2:12-13, which Guthrie thinks might be an early Christian hymn, focused, you remember, on the need for faithfulness to Christ if we are to be owned by Him at the Last Judgment. Church folk must not only know the gospel, they must be unashamed of it and live it out practically in faith before a watching world. Christians need reminding that the Christian life is serious.

Furthermore, Timothy must *keep* doing this. He must go over the truths of the gospel again and again. The congregation must be drilled in it, like soldiers. When our teachers go over the same things repeatedly, we know that we are to see those things as of great importance.

Some of the truths of Christianity do not find ready acceptance, especially in the contemporary Western world. We think of matters such as the deity of Christ, the exclusiveness of the way of salvation, the need for repentance, heaven and hell. Church leaders must persist in teaching such difficult matters. It is possible to build a church in which everyone is happy, where there is much levity, but which is little more than a social club. It's just about keeping everyone comfortable. But this falls short of resilient ministry. It's a compromised ministry. There's no salt, no gospel edge!

The church must be warned

'Warn them before God against quarreling about words; it is of no value and only ruins those who listen.' (2:14)

Christian doctrines are precious and there is a certain intellectual satisfaction in systematic theology and seeing how truths fit together. But Jesus warns even sound churches about the dangers of hearing His words but failing to put them into practice. This is the way of the foolish man who built his house upon the sand (Matt. 7:26-27). They need warning that Christian teaching is not about splitting hairs over doctrinal niceties and winning an intellectual battle of words. The Christian life is more than simply knowing the truth down to the details. It is about living for Christ. It is about a life of love. It is about saving immortal souls from eternal ruin. The fact that Paul says they must be warned *before God* shows how serious this is.

Genuine resilience is Scriptural (2:15-19)

'Do your best to present yourself to God as one approved, a workman who does not need to be ashamed and who correctly handles the word of truth.' (2:15)

True teaching is straight

True teaching comes from correctly handling God's Word, *the Word of truth*. The words 'correctly handles' come from the idea of cutting something straight. Think of a Roman road. We were up near the city of York not long ago, famous for its history. There was a road straight as an arrow for miles on the way out to the home where we were staying. Of course, we were told, 'This is an old Roman road.' We are reminded of the Scripture promise: 'Trust in the Lord with all your heart... in all your ways acknowledge him, and he will make your paths straight.' (Prov. 3:6) Timothy was to teach the Scriptures in a manner that follows the straight path of the gospel to the Lord Jesus, and leads to faith, love and godliness— without deviating.

What is the Old Testament about? It is about Christ (Luke 24:27). 'The holy Scriptures... are able to make you wise for salvation through faith in Christ Jesus.' (3:15) The law points to His perfect holiness, the sacrifices to His perfect sacrifice, the priesthood to His present intercession for us, the miracles point to His power to change our lives.

We are not in the pulpit to show off our academic prowess or make God's Word say what we would like it to say. We are there to make it say what God says as clearly as we can.

False teaching is crooked

'Avoid godless chatter, because those who indulge in it will become more and more ungodly. Their teaching will spread like gangrene. Among them are Hymenaeus and Philetus, who have wandered away from the truth. They say the resurrection has already taken place and destroy the faith of some.' (2:16-18)

By contrast to true teaching, Hymenaeus (see 1 Timothy 1:20) and Philetus had left the straight path of Scripture and 'wandered away' (2:18). A wandering path is crooked. It meanders all over the place.

The message of the false teachers denied a future resurrection and so focused on this world. In his first letter to Timothy, Paul mentioned false teachers who quarrel about words and think that godliness is a means to financial gain (1 Tim. 6:3-10). It may have been akin to the modern prosperity gospel, which dupes so many.

Paul likens false teaching to 'gangrene' (2:17) and he's making two points. *First,* it makes people spiritually sick. It makes them increasingly 'godless' instead of godly (2:16). *Second,* like gangrene, false teaching often spreads quickly. The sinful heart readily accepts it because it concerns itself with this present world, which is what the unconverted mind is naturally fixed on. And notice, because a 'Christian' teaching spreads quickly, it does not mean the Holy Spirit is at work.

Teaching to withstand false teaching

Mention of how the false teaching was spreading rapidly might well have added to Timothy's discouragement. So Paul comes in with level-headed advice: 'Nevertheless, God's solid foundation stands firm, sealed with this inscription: "The Lord knows those who are his," and, "Everyone who confesses the name of the Lord must turn away from wickedness".' (2:19).

Paul encourages us to scriptural resilience by reminding us of a scriptural story. We must not be shaken or discouraged when we see false teaching prevailing. God will save His true people—the elect (2:10). The two quotations in 2:19 probably reference Numbers 16, where we find the story of the rebellion of Korah and his followers against Moses.

In that situation, the Lord was well able to differentiate between the true and the false. The people were told to 'move away' from Moses' opponents and were saved in doing so as the earth opened and swallowed the rebels. We are not to be discouraged. We are to bear in mind the twin truths of God's sovereignty and human responsibility taught in Scripture. God's sovereignty means that God will deal with the heretics but will keep those who are His—He knows us. But simultaneously, we have the responsibility not to play with evil. Those who are God's will take warning and move away from it. They will 'turn away from wickedness' (2:19).

Here we see why true resilience is scriptural. *First*, it stands on the truths of Scripture. *Secondly,* Scripture provides us with the truths which will brace us to stand in the face of false teaching. *Thirdly*, only a church which is founded on Bible truth is worth building. This is what a true church leader continually bounces back to in order to continue building. A leader who is building any other kind of 'church' is wasting his time. He may be building, but God isn't.

Genuine resilience is sincere (2:20-22)

Have you ever come home from ministering somewhere, perhaps after a long drive, really hungry and the first thing you are going to do when you get in is cook yourself some scrambled eggs or a bacon sandwich? You arrive and eagerly go into the kitchen only to find the grill pan and all the other pans have been used by others in the house. There they are in the sink and the washing up has not been done!

Paul mixes his metaphors a little here, but it's that kind of scenario that is in his mind as he writes: 'In a large house there are articles not only of gold and silver, but also of wood and clay; some are for noble purposes and some for ignoble. If a man cleanses himself from the latter, he will be an instrument for noble purposes, made holy, useful to the Master and prepared to do any good work.' (2:20-21)

Without going into the complexities and slippage of metaphor in these verses, the straightforward thrust is that Timothy's aim must be to be ready for the Master's use. That means holiness. It means being clean for service. For

95

church leaders, it means not being mere pulpiteers living a double life, but rather ministering with a sincere desire for Christ and His kingdom.

What does that mean in practice? Paul tells us: 'Flee the evil desires of youth, and pursue righteousness, faith, love and peace, along with those who call on the Lord out of a pure heart.' (2:22) A pure heart means sincerity. True resilience is out of a heart which has a genuine single-mindedness to serve the Lord. For young Timothy that means avoiding the evil desires of youth.

With hormones raging in our younger years, that expression could well refer to sexual lust. Adultery is just one of the pitfalls in this area of temptation. The pastor is not called to be promiscuous but to be pure.

With the advent of online technology, young ministers and those not so young might have begun to dabble in internet pornography. They see it as a quick fix of excitement and comfort amid the daily battle. But it is to be avoided like the plague. Pornography is not only addictive, it actually makes male sexual arousal much more difficult, and is producing a generation of young men who are hopeless in the bedroom. Marriages fall apart because of it. Young minister be warned. But, of course, it is not simply that pornography has detrimental effects, it is that it is sinful and wrong in the sight of a holy God. There is grace and forgiveness, but we are meant to be holy men who direct our sexual drives along paths which are pleasing to God. To preach holiness to others when we are playing with porn is hypocrisy of which a pastor should be ashamed.

But the 'evil desires of youth' could be more directly connected with Timothy's teaching and its motives. There are youthful passions tied up with a teaching ministry. There is the impatience to be a somebody and to be a platform speaker at prestigious conferences. There is the hankering of the new young minister to put his mark on the church by rubbishing what the previous minister had achieved. There is the love of dispute and winning arguments—mighty king of the blogosphere! Or there is the enticement to teach novelties, which no one has heard before and amaze everyone. There are men who want a name as the soundest and most zealous. And to show they are soundest, they have no qualms about picking quarrels. Yes, there is a place for rightly defending the gospel against heresy, but these men are actually concerned to make a reputation for themselves.

And men can persevere in that lifelong quest for reputation. There is a determination and doggedness in the search for fame and name which is almost miraculous. They keep working at it come what may. But this is not true resilience. Their service has certain qualities of true resilience, but in reality it is counterfeit. It's all about serving self in ministry.

Run a mile from all of this. Paul is saying, 'Repeat after me, "I don't want to serve self, but sincerely serve my Master!"' It is this kind of resilience Paul is looking for.

Genuine resilience is sympathetic (2:23-26)

Unlike our hard-headed friend in the railway carriage, mentioned by Spurgeon, Christ-like resilience goes with compassion.

> *Don't have anything to do with foolish and stupid arguments, because you know they produce quarrels. And the Lord's servant must not quarrel; instead he must be kind to everyone, able to teach, not resentful. Those who oppose him he must gently instruct, in the hope that God will grant them repentance leading them to a knowledge of the truth, and that they will come to their senses and escape from the trap of the devil, who has taken them captive to do his will. (2:23-26)*

There is an emphasis here again on being the Lord's servant, and on avoiding needless quarrels which will disturb the unity of the congregation. But as we think about what resilience should look like we will pick up on three things. The Lord's man should aim at being kind (2:24), gentle (2:25) and hopeful (2:25).

Kind

'And the Lord's servant must not quarrel; instead he must be kind to everyone, able to teach, not resentful.' (2:24)

The command to be kind comes amidst the need of avoiding needless quarrels in the church. 'A gentle answer turns away wrath, but a harsh word stirs up anger.' (Prov. 15:1). And it also comes in the context of not being resentful. This includes learning to forgive those who have hurt you. And people do hurt you in the ministry. We are to forgive because, in Christ, God forgave us!

There is a story of John Wesley crossing the Atlantic on one of his visits to America in the days when America was still ruled by the British. On the ship was Mr Oglethorpe on his way to become the governor of Savannah, Georgia. One day there was a great commotion in the governor's cabin and Wesley went to see what the problem was.

A servant had drunk his master's bottle of wine. The governor intended to have him flogged. Wesley pleaded for leniency and forgiveness for the servant. But Mr Oglethorpe replied, 'I never forgive.' 'Your honour, then I hope you never sin!' said Wesley. This made the governor think again. With a renewed humility he approached Wesley, 'Alas, Sir, I do sin, and I have sinned in what I have said; for your sake he shall be forgiven.'[2] Our sins, and the Cross of Christ we preach, should make us kind.

Gentle

'Those who oppose him he must gently instruct…' (2:25)

The instruction concerning kindness comes in the context of trying to teach opponents. It has often been said that we can win the argument but lose the person. It is meekness which wins people. Very often people listen first not to our arguments but to our hearts and our attitude towards them. If you want to truly win an argument, you need to be a winsome person.

And that required gentleness is more likely to emerge in us if we realise our opponents are actually human. They have feelings too! And elsewhere Paul reminds us that our real opponent is not them, but the devil (2:26; Eph. 6:12). Caught in error, they are humans who are like poor animals caught in a net, or birds who cannot escape sticky bird-lime daubed on the branches of trees where they land to trap them. Understanding this kindles sympathy and a gentle approach even as they are being used to do the devil's will.

---

2. Philip De Courcy, *Emergency Rations* (Christian Focus, 2017), p. 68.

Hopeful

'… in the hope that God will grant them repentance leading to a knowledge of the truth, and that they will come to their senses and escape from the trap of the devil, who has taken them captive to do his will.' (2:25-26)

We engage opponents, not to score points or to justify ourselves but with the loving hope that God will use our words to bring them to repentance. We love them and want them to realise they have been wrong. We want them to come to their senses, back to Christ. We follow a Saviour who, as His enemies were crucifying Him, prayed, 'Father, forgive them, for they do not know what they are doing.' (Luke 23:34). And there is a sense in which every unbeliever and anti-Christian opponent does not know what they are doing because they are captive to the devil, not in their right mind. And we can be hopeful of change in people because our Lord Jesus Christ is stronger than the devil. Even the demon-possessed 'Legion' was returned to his right mind (Luke 8:35).

A serious, scriptural, sincere man who shows sympathy through being kind, gentle and hopeful makes a good pastor. And churches need men who will be like that, Summer, Winter, Autumn and Spring, year after year after year. That is what true resilience should look like.

How can a Christian leader know this kind of genuine resilience for Christ? How can he walk this path amid the storms and battles? There is a golden thread which runs through our passage which I think shows us the way. It is the golden thread of God-centredness. We cannot do this without God.

- In the church, there should be an awareness of God's presence. Timothy's ministry to his congregation is to be 'before God' (2:14).
- In the study, there should be an awareness of God. The pastor's preparation for preaching should be as 'present[ing]' himself and his work 'to God' (2:15). 'Would I say this if Christ Himself were here?'
- In his heart, there should be an awareness of God. His great aim should be to be 'useful to the Master' in every possible way (2:21).
- In the counselling room, there needs to be a sense of God. His ministry, as he deals with various difficult individuals, is out of hope in God, trusting God to be at work in these folk (2:25).

Paul's strident recommissioning of Timothy, which is a highlight later in the Epistle, strikes the same note. It is as if both the apostle and his protégé are standing in the very throne room of God: 'In the presence of God and of Christ Jesus, who will judge the living and the dead, and in view of his appearing and his kingdom, I give you this charge: preach the word' (4:1-2a).

A right attitude in our resilience comes from a constant awareness of God. Let such words as these ever be in the pastor's mind: 'My ministry is not for me, or even to please other people. It is for God. This church is not our church. It is God's church. I am not my own. I am the Lord's servant. By His grace I do my best for Him!'

Exercise for those in ministry

There is much in 2 Timothy concerning being clear as to our priorities. The soldier is not to get entangled in civilian affairs (2:4). The Lord's servant is not to quarrel or be resentful (2:24), but to put trying to teach and win others at the top of his 'to do' list. Timothy is to preach the word in season and out of season (4:2).

Think through your ministry in terms of what Scripture says about your role and the needs of your church. Try to write a list of priorities and set them in order.

How can being clear as to your priorities save ministers from burn-out? What, in your church or in your own character, is likely to pull you away from sticking to those priorities? Pray and ask God to help you to have wisdom with respect to your ministry priorities.

6
Why the Increasing Need for Resilience?

But mark this: There will be terrible times in the last days. People will be lovers of themselves, lovers of money, boastful, proud, abusive, disobedient to their parents, ungrateful, unholy, without love, unforgiving, slanderous, without self-control, brutal, not lovers of the good, treacherous, rash, conceited, lovers of pleasure rather than lovers of God—having a form of godliness but denying its power. Have nothing to do with them.

They are the kind who worm their way into homes and gain control over weak-willed women, who are loaded down with sins and are swayed by all kinds of evil desires, always learning but never able to acknowledge the truth. Just as Jannes and Jambres opposed Moses, so also these men oppose the truth—men of depraved minds, who, as far as the faith is concerned, are rejected. But they will not get very far because, as in the case of those men, their folly will be clear to everyone.

You, however, know all about my teaching, my way of life, my purpose, faith, patience, love, endurance, persecutions, sufferings—what kinds of things happened to me in Antioch, Iconium and Lystra, the persecutions I endured. Yet the Lord rescued me from all of them. In fact, everyone who wants to live a godly life in Christ

Jesus will be persecuted, while evil men and impostors will go from bad to worse, deceiving and being deceived.

But as for you, continue in what you have learned and become convinced of, because you know those from whom you learned it, and how from infancy you have known the holy Scriptures, which are able to make you wise for salvation through faith in Christ Jesus. All Scripture is God-breathed and is useful for teaching, rebuking, correcting and training in righteousness, so that the man of God may be thoroughly equipped for every good work.

In the presence of God and of Christ Jesus, who will judge the living and the dead, and in view of his appearing and his kingdom, I give you this charge: Preach the word; be prepared in season and out of season; correct, rebuke and encourage – with great patience and careful instruction. For the time will come when men will not put up with sound doctrine. Instead, to suit their own desires, they will gather around them a great number of teachers to say what their itching ears want to hear. They will turn their ears away from the truth and turn aside to myths. But you, keep your head in all situations, endure hardship, do the work of an evangelist, discharge all the duties of your ministry. (2 Tim. 3:1–4:5)

The 2003 film *Goodbye Lenin* is both a tragedy and a comedy. It is set in East Berlin and begins in 1989 just as Communism in Europe is about to fall. Soon the Berlin Wall will be demolished.

A son, Alex, and a daughter, Ariane, live in a flat with their mother, Christiane. Their father seems to have abandoned the family, escaping to the West some ten years earlier. Deserted by her spouse, Christiane has become a fervent supporter of the ruling Communist Party, looking upon the Party almost as a surrogate husband. But times are changing. People want freedom, especially the younger generation, and Alex gets involved in anti-government demonstrations.

As she passes by one such demonstration, Christiane witnesses her son being arrested and, seeing this, she suffers a near fatal heart attack and falls into a coma. Shortly afterward, the Berlin Wall comes down, the Communist leader, Erich Honecker, resigns and East Berlin embraces capitalism. After some months in hospital, Christiane wakes up but is very weak. Doctors warn that any shock or trauma might cause another heart attack that would be likely to kill her.

Her son, Alex, realises that the discovery that her beloved Communism has collapsed might be too much for his mother to bear and, having got her home, he decides he must maintain the pretence that everything is as it was for his now bedridden mother. With mother in mind, at home, he and his sister go to extraordinary lengths to carry on the delusion that they still live in the Communist German Democratic Republic. This is where the comedy begins. The siblings dress in their old clothes. Western products are repackaged in old East German jars. With the help of a friend, old East German broadcasts are re-edited into 'news' on the radio. His mother's accidentally seeing a sign for Coca-Cola is explained in terms of the East German State taking in refugees from the West and the government trying to make them feel at home.

The world has changed, but the pretence is pursued that it hasn't. Of course, such a pretence is only possible for so long. Christiane begins to suspect what has really happened. She dies just a couple of days before the formal reunification of Germany.

The church in a changed world

Today, like Christiane, many Christians are having to wake up to a reality they don't much care for. They may not have been in a long-term coma, but they've been asleep spiritually, insulated in the Christian bubble of church, conferences and Christian books, somehow in denial about what's happened in secular society over the last few decades. Now they are at last becoming conscious of the fact that the world has changed dramatically.

Whereas Christians used to be thought a bit nutty but basically good folk, dependable citizens, we are increasingly regarded as a bad influence in society. Christian marriage, which was the foundation of Western society a generation ago, is now ignored or even despised. Freedom of religion and freedom of speech are under attack in the West. Our world has morphed almost out of all recognition. Things which once were almost universally regarded as bad are now celebrated as good. It is a woeful situation (Isa. 5:20). Many people, including those in positions of power in politics and the media, are now very antagonistic towards Christianity and the churches. A cultural revolution has taken place. The old order has gone.

The thesis of this chapter is that Christians and Christian leaders must wake up to the fact of this change. They must realise, also, that they will need to be increasingly resilient in order to stand and be faithful in this increasingly hostile environment.

The encouragement, however, is that the Bible knows all about our situation. This section of 2 Timothy both predicts it and explains what is happening. In his advice to Timothy, Paul makes it clear to us what we must do. We will gather the gist of what he says under five headings.

Recognize the times (3:1-5)

Paul begins to warn Timothy as follows: 'But mark this: There will be terrible times in the last days.'

In Scripture, the last days are the whole period between Christ's First and Second Comings. We, ourselves, live in the last days. And in that period, Paul tells us, there will be terrible times. The sense appears to be that it will not be consistently bad, but there will be periods of great trouble and moral evil. Some Christians feel that these terrible times may be more intense and more prolonged as the Second Coming draws near (3:13).

As we read Paul's description of what these terrible times look like, it is not hard to come to the conclusion that we are entering, or have already entered, such a time now. The church needs to recognise this.

What's the cause?

A society is defined by what it loves. Its fundamental desires determine its outlook, its values, whom it treats well and whom it disdains. What it loves, it will legitimize, work towards and institutionalise.

Paul's opening headline concerning the 'terrible times' tells us: 'People will be lovers of themselves, lovers of money...' (3:2) It is not rocket science for us to identify ourselves and our generation. We invented the 'selfie'. We live in a consumer-culture. We love money because we can use it to get whatever we want for ourselves. He goes on to give a list of sins which characterise the terrible times.

Paul's closing summary of these sins describes people as 'lovers of pleasure rather than lovers of God' (3:4b). Of course this is true. Being lovers of self in the end boils down to being lovers of pleasure. And that leads to a secular society which rejects God. Self is god and will brook no rivals. And it leads to all those sins, often aggressive and abusive, listed in 3:2-4, which are prevalent today. Sociologists speak of the 'therapy culture' in which the whole goal is to make ourselves feel good and to continue to feel good about ourselves.

This is the trajectory on which secularism, or tacit atheism, has taken us. People think that you can do away with God and still have a decent society. But the Bible tells us otherwise and experience proves it. As society has become more secular over the last half century, it has become a more dark, lonely, fragmented and unsafe place to live. When we turn from God, we do away with any ultimate authority outside ourselves (it usually takes a society a little time to realise that). But that brings people into conflict with each other. Then the whole dynamic of claiming 'victim status' can come into play, which is such a powerful card to play in the contemporary world. The greatest 'sin' in a therapy culture is 'you've hurt me' or 'you've made me feel bad'. This is our politically correct world.

What's the effect?

As secularism puts 'feel good' at the heart of society, it turns everything upside down. It engenders a society where people are *not lovers of the good* (3:3c). '[G]ood' itself is no longer defined in classic moral terms. It is redefined in emotional or therapy categories. Good is what feels good.

What should be loved as 'good' is not loved but despised. Let us take the example of parenting. In the contemporary world, parenting is no longer about children learning from parents and obeying them (because parents love them and know best by experience). That is regarded as authoritarian and bad. Parenting is now principally about making the child feel good about himself or herself. But here is the crunch point. How is a parent ever to know they have succeeded in that? The answer is, only if the child tells them. So, who is now in the driving seat of the parent-child relationship? It is the child! This is completely upside down from the way previous generations would have seen parenting.

And for quite similar reasons, Christians, who in the past were looked upon as 'good people', are now regarded with suspicion. We are told that with our moral framework to life we are authoritarian and repressive. We should not be talking about sin and the need for redemption, implying that there are right and wrong ways to live life. That makes people feel bad. We should simply be trying to affirm people in whatever they choose.

Faithful Christians find themselves as outsiders and rejects. That is hard for us. As society continues to pursue its path, we will increasingly require resilience as Christians and as Christian leaders.

What are the lessons?
There are lessons here that it would be disastrous for the church to ignore.

First, there are some negatives. It is clear that in a 'feel good' culture, where people are lovers of pleasure rather than lovers of God, pastors may have to fight hard to keep the church God-centred.

In our verses, Paul implies that these people who live for 'feel good' and affirmation can even claim to be Christians. They are those *having a form of godliness but denying its power* (3:5a). There are folk who may love religious aesthetics or going to church and a liturgy but do not want anything to do with the moral demands of the new birth. There are those who feel lifted in an emotional worship service with tremendous 'gospel' music and singing but just want to fit in with the rest of society otherwise. There are those who love niceness rather than truth.

But if such people are allowed influence in the churches, their attitude will soon be such as effectively sidelines the God of the Bible and turns Christian virtues upside down. The apostle tells Timothy and us to *have nothing to do with them* (3:5). Do not accept them. Do not allow them into your pulpits. Do not let them into church membership.

That is all very well, but we have to realise that leaders who take Paul's command seriously will be given a rough ride. We can imagine the kind of angry comments faithful pastors will have to face. 'How can you possibly not admit people to the Lord's table? How unloving! We are meant to be inclusive. You are a disgrace to Christianity!' Pastors will need to be resilient.

Second, there is a big positive. The situation for Christians and Christian leaders in the contemporary world may well be unprecedented in the history of the church. Our fathers and grandfathers and those before them never knew, or perhaps could not even imagine, such things. And, unless God intervenes in a most remarkable way, it is unlikely that things are going to change any time soon. It would be easy for us to panic. But it is not only encouraging that Scripture knows all about what we face, it is greatly encouraging that this implies that God knows what we face and He will have a path through this for His people. We can trust Him.

Understand the opposition (3:6-9)

Out of this secular/'feel good' culture will emerge teachers who 'oppose the truth' (3:8). Paul uses the Exodus story as the background to his thinking here as he refers to Moses and Pharaoh's magicians who opposed him. The battle for truth has a long history. Then it was the gods of Egypt versus the Lord. Now it is the gods of self and money against the Lord. Battling against error is draining and hard.

The subtlety of the false teachers

These teachers can be religious or secular. They are devious. They 'worm their way into homes' (3:6a). They target the tired and the vulnerable. Paul mentions 'weak-willed women' (3:6). There are many sensible women with robust characters. But false teachers tend to pass them by. Their aim is to 'gain control'. In other words they want to tell people what to think rather than teaching them to think for themselves. That's why their followers are always learning but never able to come to firm conclusions (3:7).

Whereas the false teachers of Timothy's day have been and gone, and we could now talk about the cults who go from door to door trying to gain entrance with their heresies, I can't help but think of the TV and the internet as I read these verses. These bits of technology slip into our sitting rooms under the guise of providing entertainment and being informative. And it's true, we need to relax sometimes. But false teachers often use them. We press the button on the remote or the laptop in the evening when we are tired from a day's work. And there, not thinking straight, we are fed secular lies by the lorry load. It is, of course, a careful mix of truth and error, humanity and immorality, which enthralls the audience to the outlook of the secular media elite. The 'feel good' culture pervades everything presented.

The issue is that these teachers oppose truth (3:8). Ultimately, that means that there is no discussion, no listening to both sides of the argument. For example, I have never seen a TV programme which presents the medical facts concerning sexually transmitted diseases in the light of both permissiveness and chastity.

But it's not just the media. In universities we have witnessed even fervent feminists de-platformed because, as a speaker they doubt the current politically correct line on transgender issues. There has been the creation of 'safe-zones' where nothing challenging is presented to students. Free thought and speech are slipping away. Seeking the truth is going out of fashion. And, in particular, there is the suppressing truth about God.

In schools there is no presentation of both sides of the argument on creation and evolution. There is no evenhandedness. Science is meant to be about evidence. The evidence of the fossils is that suddenly all the basic forms of animal life appear without precursors. It is called 'The Cambrian explosion'. The major categories appear before the multiplication of small differences among species. Darwin's theory predicts the opposite. But there is to be no argument. Or again, we often hear that some bacteria acquire resistance to certain antibiotics. This is presented as conclusive proof of evolution. But what is not said is that such adaptation merely utilises existing genetic information within the bacteria; no new genetic information has been created, which is the crucial necessity for Darwinian evolution. The evidence says there is an adaptation (microevolution) but that comes out of the existing complexity of the organisms. It is an 'evolution' that depends on previous design.

We are clearly living in a period when truth is opposed or suppressed in order to bolster the prevailing culture. These are the false teachers the faithful Christian pastor is up against.

The motivation of the false teachers

These teachers and those they influence are 'swayed by evil desires' (3:6). They are 'men of depraved minds' (3:8). In other words, it is their desires which control their thinking. People like to think of a Sherlock Holmes type of character as their ideal. Everything is clinical. The intellectual detective carefully and impartially weighs all the evidence and then draws unassailable conclusions which are absolutely rigorous. Indeed, that is a great ideal to seek to emulate. But the truth is that none of us, left to ourselves as fallen human beings, are like that. It is a myth. We are not motivated by a noble quest for the truth. We are motivated, ultimately, by naturally wayward attitudes and selfish desires and we are quite willing to oppose the truth where we deem that necessary.

In his very worthwhile book *The Righteous Mind,* moral psychologist Jonathan Haidt torpedoes the prevailing myth of unbiased thinking.[1] He asks the reader to think of a large elephant on which is sitting a small rider. The elephant represents our innate intuitions and desires. The rider is our intellect, our thinking. If the elephant sways or stumbles, the rider always acts to correct the elephant and keep him upright. Our visceral intuitions are the seat of stability and feeling okay about ourselves. If they are upset, then our very identity is in jeopardy. So when the elephant is unbalanced by something, the rider reacts so as not to let the elephant fall. What this means for us is that, when faced with challenging ideas or evidence, we are not neutral. Our first reaction will be for our intellect to come up with arguments to validate the *status quo*, our intuitions and desires. According to Haidt, the research shows that this is a fair picture of how we operate.

So, if the Bible is correct when it speaks of human beings as corrupted creatures, enthralled to sin and self-centredness, we are hardly likely to find a balanced and careful approach to truth. This exposes the true motivation of false teachers. According to Paul, they are

---

1. Jonathan Haidt, *The Righteous Mind: Why good people are divided by politics and religion* (Penguin, 2013).

swayed by their desires. We are no longer dealing with open minds and fair arguments.

The 'feel good' society will always come up with reasoning so as to validate sin. And the validation of what the Bible labels sin has dominated much of the social history of the West for the last seventy years. Once again, we see why in these 'terrible times' Christian teachers will be opposed and will need resilience.

Prepare for persecution (3:10-13)

In contrast to these devious teachers stands Paul, Christ's apostle:

> *You, however, know all about my teaching, my way of life, my purpose, faith, patience, love, endurance, persecutions, sufferings— what kinds of things happened to me in Antioch, Iconium, and Lystra, the persecutions I endured. Yet the Lord rescued me from all of them. In fact, everyone who wants to live a godly life in Christ Jesus will be persecuted, while evil men and impostors will go from bad to worse, deceiving and being deceived.*

Why persecution?

Paul's teaching is truth. It is all about the Lord Jesus Christ who told us, 'I am the way, and the truth, and the life' (John 14:6a). The gospel we preach comes not from ourselves, influenced by sin, but from God. By contrast, false teachers, and the secular society from which they emerge and which they influence, oppose the truth (2 Tim. 3:8). There follows, therefore, an inevitable confrontation, and, because Paul's way of life seeks to live out the truth (3:10)—the truth that leads to godliness (Titus 1:1)—then he suffers (3:11a). His preaching leads straight to persecution. As we have already noted on several occasions, Timothy was from Lystra himself. He knew what Paul refers to in verse 11. He may well have been an eyewitness of Paul's stoning by the people of his home town and being left for dead outside the town gate.

Paul warns that 'everyone who wants to live a godly life in Christ Jesus will be persecuted' (3:12). I don't think Paul is necessarily saying that godly Christians will always be persecuted wherever they are found throughout the last days. I think that what he is saying pertains particularly in the 'terrible times' which opens our section in 3:1. He is warning us that, in the godless, 'feel good' societies which he describes in 3:2-5, persecution will inevitably break out.

Christians have not really suffered persecution in the UK for a couple of centuries because society has been so influenced by the gospel. The great revivals of the eighteenth century, under Wesley, Whitefield and others, transformed our islands. In Victorian times, the United Kingdom became a great base for worldwide missionary effort. Not everyone was a Christian, but there was a Christian consensus which ruled the outlook of the nation. But now that is waning. And we must prepare for trouble. Pastors must begin to think about how best to organise and care for churches during terrible times.

What sort of persecution is likely to come? It will probably not be any state-sponsored violence. The horrific inhumanity of the Jewish Holocaust has left a legacy, which still protects us. No government would want to be compared to the Nazis. But we may well be exposed to violence from special interest groups who oppose Christianity to whom governments will turn a blind eye. There are violent people out there who may attack individual Christians or churches if they think they can get away with it.

But more likely state persecution will come in other forms. Already we have seen Christians facing reprimands at work for seeking to share their faith. Christian magistrates have been forced to step down because it is known that they favour traditional marriage. Preachers might well face fines or even imprisonment for declaring truths which society does not like.

The question will be whether the churches can stand. Will a congregation stand with their pastor if he is questioned by the authorities about his sermon? Or will they distance themselves from him and say, 'Well, he is a bit extreme'? Will Christians be prepared to stay in a church pilloried by the press and given a bad reputation for its stance on marriage or on Christ as the only way of salvation? Will they keep meeting and coming to church on Sundays through a crowd of TV cameras or photographers from the national newspapers?

And, if people in the congregation do begin to distance themselves from the man in the pulpit, how will he feel? Will he understand and still love and care? If what we are imagining here becomes something of a reality, it is going to take leaders of great resilience to bring the churches through.

What hope?

Under the influence of the secularised media and other false teachers, society is likely to get worse before it gets better. 'Evil men and impostors will go from bad to worse, deceiving and being deceived' (3:13). But it is not all gloom and doom. God does not allow these terrible times and the false teachers who fan the flames of persecution to go on forever (3:9). And we have something the world does not have. We have a living, Almighty Lord. As he listed his sufferings for Christ, Paul makes sure he encourages Timothy too. He says he has experienced many persecutions, 'yet the Lord rescued me from all of them' (3:11c).

How do we prepare for persecution? We face the threat. But we renew our faith in God. He is able to keep us. He is able to do more than we ask or imagine (Eph. 3:20).

Stand on Scripture (3:14-16)

Paul sees that, as always, upholding the Word of God will be the crucial battlefront during these terrible times. So he exhorts his young friend: 'But as for you, continue in what you have learned and become convinced of…' He is talking about Scripture (3:15- 16).

Those who stand on the Word of God will be rejected by a corrupt and self-adoring society. This has always been the experience of God's faithful servants.

- Noah warned the world of coming judgment but was simply ignored. He, no doubt, realised how few there were who followed him, and perhaps was caused to wonder if such a small minority could ever be right while the vast majority were wrong. But he continued to preach and was vindicated.
- Elijah was accused of being a troubler of the nation by King Ahab (1 Kings 18:17). That tactic is sometimes

used to try to silence us. 'Everybody is happy with what is going on. Why don't you evangelicals just leave people alone to get on with their own lives?' Doubts can creep in for the preacher. But Elijah did not back down.

- Jeremiah was in the line of fire and faced tremendous opposition as he called his nation to repentance and warned that otherwise the Babylonians would be sent by God to destroy Jerusalem and lead them in chains into exile. False prophets enjoyed preaching more acceptable messages and gained approval. By contrast, Jeremiah was imprisoned and thrown into a boggy pit. But he didn't change his message.

A society in love with itself will try all kinds of tactics to drag us down and keep us from preaching the Word of God. And Paul recognises the power which fear, ostracism and persecution can wield. Like an isolated victim bamboozled and beaten under the lights by secret police, we can feel tempted to agree to things which we know are simply not true. They can pressure us to deny what we know to be right, what we have become convinced of! 'But don't give in!' says Paul. Be resilient to the last.

Why resist?

Paul gives three reasons for continuing to stand on Scripture.

First, he says concerning the truth of Scripture, 'because you know those from whom you learned it' (3:14b). With the mention of Timothy's infancy in 3:15 and the references to his mother and grandmother in 1:5, it must be principally those two women, Eunice and Lois, whom

119

Paul has in mind. These two act in the role of those who give testimonials as to the truth and goodness of Scripture as their lives show the good influence the Bible has had on them. They are rather like character witnesses in court as Scripture is put in the dock. Their good and godly lives show the blessed effect that God's Word produces in those who receive its teaching into their hearts. This speaks of the goodness and validity of the Bible.

Of course, Timothy also learned much from Paul himself. He is probably included in 3:14b. Timothy knows Paul's way of life (3:10). So Paul is next in the witness box on the side of Scripture. 'Timothy,' Paul is saying, 'you know and love your mum, your grandma, and me. You have been blessed through us. Realise that our characters have been shaped by Scripture.'

Here is the first reason not to give up on the Bible. Perhaps there are Christian people we have known whom we have loved and looked up to, who could take the witness box with Eunice, Lois and Paul for the benefits and truth of Scripture and of whom we should take notice?

Second, Paul reasons with Timothy not to move away from Scripture because 'from infancy you have known the holy Scriptures, which are able to make you wise for salvation through faith in Christ Jesus' (3:15). There is a contrast here, which we must not miss, between this verse and 3:5. A church dominated by therapy culture has a form of godliness but lacks God's power (3:5). But Scripture is able—has the power—to save us and change our lives (3:15). The same Greek word, *dunamis,* is used in both verses. Churches which deny Scripture will lack power. This should not surprise us. Elsewhere,

Paul famously describes the message of the gospel, which Scripture conveys, as 'the power of God for the salvation of everyone who believes' (Rom. 1:16). To move away from Scripture is to throw away the church's power.

The implication is that the way of salvation (through Christ) is taught in Scripture and there is no other way. To swerve away from Scripture is to swerve away from Christ and so to take the broad road that leads to destruction.

The Christ of Scripture is the true Christ—all others are invented fantasies. This Christ is the only way for sinners to escape hell and gain heaven. It may be a tough road now, but it is far better in the long run to stay on the narrow road that leads to life.

With its background text in Acts 4:12, the chorus of Graham Kendrick's song 'Above the Clash of Creeds' sums up the fundamentals of the uniqueness of Christ very well:

> *There is no other way*
> *By which we must be saved*
> *His name is Jesus*
> *The only Saviour*
> *No other sinless life*
> *No other sacrifice*
> *In all creation*
> *No other way*

To be true to Jesus, we have to be true to His word. 'If anyone is ashamed of me and my words in this adulterous and sinful generation, the Son of Man will be ashamed of him when he comes in his Father's glory with the holy angels' (Mark 8:38).

121

Third, Paul remonstrates with Timothy to hold on to Scripture because Scripture is God's word. 'All Scripture is God-breathed and is useful for teaching, rebuking, correcting and training in righteousness, so that the man of God may be thoroughly equipped for every good work' (3:16-17).

Paul's point is: 'Don't depart from Scripture, Timothy, because as a pastor you will only be helpful to people as you relay God's own word to them.' And that is what Scripture is—the word that God has spoken out just as we speak by breathing out over our vocal chords. And the word spoken by the eternal God is eternally relevant.

It will equip you to be able to do your job of helping God's people in these difficult times. Dig deeply into it. It will make you a true prophet for your times. That is the implication of Paul using the Old Testament phrase 'man of God' so often used of prophets like Samuel (1 Sam. 9:6, etc.). Human ideas are faulty and passing and cannot sustain God's people. They need the word of the eternal God for the good of their immortal souls.

And notice that Paul deploys a majority of negative concepts when it comes to how Timothy will have to make use of Scripture. Scripture can encourage and excite and delight. But Paul speaks of rebuking the rebellious, and correcting the ignorant, and training the spiritually lazy. He is expecting that the teaching ministry will be a battle during the terrible times of the last days.

In commending Scripture, Paul has addressed Timothy as a man, as a Christian and as a pastor.

- 'As a man, recognise how Scripture has motivated your family and me to love and care for you' (3:14).

122

- 'As a Christian, recognize that Scripture alone shows us the gospel of Christ which is the power of God for salvation' (3:15).
- 'As a pastor, recognize that Scripture alone can equip you for your task of helping people' (3:16-17).

So continue in what you have learned, rest on Scripture. And that leads to our last section.

Complete the task (4:1-5)

As a self-absorbed world thinks about 'me-time' the apostle contemplates 'end-time'. We have already quoted Jesus' words about what will occur at His Second Coming. The Second Coming is very much in Paul's mind as he reaches the climax of his exhortation to Timothy. We can become very fearful of what the people of the corrupt contemporary world might think of us. But on that day of days our ministry will be exposed to the scrutiny of the Son of God in all His glory.

> *In the presence of God and of Christ Jesus, who will judge the living and the dead, and in view of his appearing and kingdom, I give you this charge: Preach the Word; be prepared in season and out of season; correct, rebuke and encourage—with great patience and careful instruction.*

'Since we are to appear before our Master to give an account,' Paul is saying, 'let's make sure we do our best to complete the task assigned to us as pastors and preachers.' That's the thrust of these verses. Christians, and especially Christian teachers, will face a judgment in which they will either be rewarded or rebuked by Christ Himself (1 Cor. 3:12-15; James 3:1). Having served Christ faithfully,

Paul is looking forward to a crown of righteousness on that day (4:8). He wants Timothy to be able to look forward to the same accolade on that awesome day. We are reminded that a call to Christian ministry is a matter of enormous gravity. What would it be for Christ to have called us to the work, but then for us to down tools and walk away? Timothy is not to give up on ministry but to keep going. Paul's charge can be seen as having seven elements.

- Preach the Word. The wording is very abrupt. It implies that Timothy is in crisis with regard to his ministry and must make a decision. He must take positive steps with definite resolve to preach despite opposition.
- Be prepared. The idea of 'in season and out of season' here is that the pastor does not go missing when there is need. Yes, there is a proper place for rest, but not when duty calls. Preach whether people listen or not. Preach in times of blessing. Preach when there seems to be no fruit.
- Correct. There will be many false ideas flying around, even in churches, during these terrible times. Put people right.
- Rebuke. Wrong ideas will lead to wrong behaviour. That must be opposed when it is found among God's people. The pastor must not shy away from discipline and being straight with people.
- Encourage. The terrible times will be very discouraging for Christian people. The preacher must seek to cheer his people with the grace of God in the gospel and so spur them on.

- Be patient. The pastor is not to give up on people. He is not to be harsh and censorious but to be loving and to stick at his task. People will need time. Rethinking and admitting fault is not easy for proud sinners. But persist and wait. Fruit doesn't ripen overnight.

- Be careful. There needs to be a thoroughness in the pastor's teaching. The pastor is not simply to skate over the surface in his teaching. He is to get to the heart of things. Also, he needs to be well-rounded in his teaching. God's sovereignty needs to be balanced with human responsibility. Heaven must be balanced by hell. God's free grace needs to be balanced with the call to holiness. People need the whole Bible taught rigorously.

The awesome charge of 4:1-2 must be carried out in the midst of the corrupt society described in 4:3-4 and every opportunity taken.

> *For the time will come when men will not put up with sound doctrine. Instead to suit their own desires, they will gather around them a great number of teachers to say what their itching ears want to hear. They will turn their ears away from the truth and turn aside to myths (4:3-4).*

The people of the secular, 'feel good' society only want to hear what will suit them. They are quite prepared to forfeit truth and oppose reality in order to be affirmed as people in their life choices. Even myths and made-up stories will do if they make them feel better.

Though he comes to it via a slightly different route, the Catholic thinker Charles Taylor, in his book *A Secular*

Age, sees the same phenomenon emerging in our times. Though evangelicals rightly emphasise an emotional dimension to our faith but keep it tethered to orthodox doctrine, Taylor says it is only a matter of time in society 'before the emphasis will shift more and more towards the strength and genuineness of feelings, rather than the nature of their object.' He goes so far as to see an imperative arising which says, 'Let everyone follow his/her own path of spiritual inspiration. Don't be led off yours by the allegation that it doesn't fit with some orthodoxy.'[2]

The pastor will have to work hard in such an environment to demonstrate that God's Word is truth and not made up of myths. The Bible is not just one set of myths which can easily be traded for another according to taste. It is truth. It is history. To labour to convince people of this will stretch us, both intellectually and spiritually.

But we have reality and conscience on our side. The world cannot be other than it actually is. We started our chapter by referring to the film *Goodbye Lenin*, in which out of love for his mother, a young East German man, after the events of 1989, tries to pretend that Communism still rules in their country. But eventually, of course, the pretence fails. And just so, the pretence that there is no God, no absolute truth and no one to answer to, which sustains the contemporary amoral therapy culture, is bound to fail too. It is the fool who says in his heart 'there is no God' (Ps. 14:1). That is why these terrible times

---

2. Quoted in James K. A. Smith, *How (not) to be Secular: Reading Charles Taylor* (Eerdmans, 2014), page 88.

during the last days are of limited duration. So don't give up. See your task through.

Pastoring in a 'feel good' society

The work of the pastor becomes much harder as secular society around us falls deeper into moral decay and becomes more decadent.

The problem is that the 'feel good' culture is likely to invade the churches in one way or another. My assessment is that it is already doing so. This will skew the thinking of some professing Christians and will mess up their lives. As the faithful pastor seeks to shepherd these people, it will increase his burden.

Many of us who have been in the ministry for decades have witnessed the load getting greater. As secularism has begun to dominate, much more pastoral care is required. As therapy culture takes its toll, much more is demanded of young pastors than was ever expected of previous generations of ministers. Here are just a few examples of how the work of the pastor has become more demanding.

- As congregations hang loose to God's commands, pastoral problems have become much more complicated as professing Christians stray into sins generally unheard of in former years. This can lead to an increasing need for church discipline, which no one enjoys.
- With an emphasis on leisure, the Lord's Day has been downgraded in churches. Many church members frequently take weekends away. Some churches only

meet once on Sundays. All this makes it more difficult to teach the church and show care.

- With the 'feel good' factor influencing many churches, there is an increasing pressure on pastors to make the church grow. In many ways that is good, but it can have its downside. People expect to be part of a 'successful church'. Pity the pastor who is not 'successful'. He can easily find himself on a treadmill trying desperately to produce what is expected of him.

- When folk are converted from non-church 'paganism', we must rejoice. But they often come from extremely dysfunctional backgrounds and so require an awful lot of care.

- Along with therapy culture comes a sense of entitlement and the expectation of individual attention from the pastor. Not only must he preach well, he is expected to find lots of times for one-to-ones.

- One-to-one studies no doubt have their place, but often these can mutate into a situation of dependency (or even co-dependency), which potentially gobbles even greater amounts of time.

- As therapy culture has affected Christians, church parents have felt less able to be authoritative with their children. It is a generalisation, but children seem to have become less well-behaved, making church more difficult.

- Changes in society have meant that the willing cohort of stay-at-home mums of previous years, who were happy to serve the church's work, are now in full-time employment and are no longer available. So extra responsibilities fall on the pastor, especially in smaller churches.

- There has been a societal rise in debt, long working-hours and depression, which also has seeped into the churches. This affects individuals and churches and so impacts the pastor.
- Older people are living longer and, as they become more frail, of course it is right that they need more pastoral care and attention.

This is not an exhaustive list. And some of these things have nothing to do with society going bad. But some do.

So, along with the greater antagonism there is from outside the church from the self-loving society, the needs within the church also grow and the work gets harder. And perhaps it is partly from that perspective that we need to understand Paul's closing words in this section: 'But you, keep your head in all situations, endure hardship, do the work of an evangelist, discharge all the duties of your ministry' (4:5).

The situations pastors face are likely to get more difficult. There will be a temptation under this increasing pressure to cut corners—perhaps to let go of evangelism. If pastors are going to keep their sanity, they will have to realise that they cannot do everything. They will need to keep their heads. There will need to be some prioritisation along with a sacrificial willingness to do as much as possible. Certainly, this situation calls for the pastor to be at his best. It will require a sensible sharing of the load of ministry where that is possible. But that does not mean giving vital areas of teaching and caring to inexperienced trainees and amateur preachers. Good pastoral teams will need to be built if possible.

The decaying society does bring a greater pastoral load, and this is another reason why in the terrible times of the last days, there is an increased need for resilience in church leaders.

We can summarise Paul's encouragement to Timothy in 4:5 with four watchwords for pastors ministering during the terrible times of the last days. Be sensible. Be sacrificial. Be evangelistic. Be thorough.

It's likely to get harder before it gets better. The need for resilience is likely to increase. But don't be floored by all this. Paul has warned us. So, recognise the times, understand the opposition, prepare for persecution, stand on Scripture and complete the task.

Exercise for those in ministry

In this chapter, it has been suggested that as the world has changed, the pressures on church leaders have increased. This may make us very aware of our own limitations.

What limitations must any pastor accept? What limitations must a married pastor with a family accept? What limitations must a single man in ministry accept?

Before God think through your own strengths and weaknesses and make a list of each. When can our strengths become weaknesses? When can our weaknesses become strengths?

7

The Pastor's Crown

For I am already being poured out like a drink offering, and the time has come for my departure. I have fought the good fight, I have finished the race, I have kept the faith. Now there is in store for me the crown of righteousness, which the Lord, the righteous Judge, will award to me on that day—and not only to me, but also to all who have longed for his appearing.

Do your best to come to me quickly, for Demas, because he loved this world, has deserted me and gone to Thessalonica. Crescens has gone to Galatia and Titus to Dalmatia. Only Luke is with me. Get Mark and bring him with you, because he is helpful to me in my ministry. I sent Tychicus to Ephesus. When you come, bring the cloak that I left with Carpus in Troas, and my scrolls, especially the parchments.

Alexander the metalworker did me a great deal of harm. The Lord will repay him for what he has done. You too should be on your guard against him, because he strongly opposed our message.

At my first defence, no one came to my support, but everyone deserted me. May it not be held against them. But the Lord stood at my side and gave me strength, so that through me the message might be fully proclaimed and all the Gentiles might hear it. And I was delivered from the lion's mouth. The Lord will rescue me from every evil attack and will bring me safely to his heavenly kingdom. To him be glory for ever and ever. Amen.

Greet Priscilla and Aquila and the household of Onesiphorus. Erastus stayed in Corinth, and I left Trophimus sick in Miletus. Do your best to get here before winter. Eubulus greets you, and so do Pudens, Linus, Claudia and all the brothers.

The Lord be with your spirit. Grace be with you. (2 Tim. 4:6-22)

One of the biggest questions that any human being wrestles with is 'has my life been worthwhile?' This might particularly be in a pastor's mind, especially as he comes to the end of his ministry.

Of course, secularists and atheists dismiss it as a foolish question because they see all of existence as an absurd cosmic accident. If the whole universe has no meaning, then how can our lives have any meaning or significance? They can't. Nevertheless, it is part of our image-of-God humanity that we can't help but keep on asking the question.

By contrast, the gospel teaches that our lives can count. Paul, in these verses, speaks of his life being poured out 'as a drink offering'—something which God counts as precious. Our lives can be lived in such a way as to be significant in the most profound way imaginable. We are given, in Christ, not just a possible five minutes of fame (if we're lucky) among the other temporary residents of planet Earth, but the 'well done' from the Judge of all things, whose assessments are unchallengeable, true and eternally meaningful. The pouring out of our lives in service leads to an everlasting crown bestowed by God 'who was and is and is to come'. Paul refers to it here in our final passage from 2 Timothy as 'the crown of righteousness'.

It is essential that pastors and Christian workers keep their eyes fixed on that ultimate reward. This is especially the case as, like Paul here, we come to the conclusion of our ministry. However, pastors just starting out on the work need to keep their eyes on the crown too if they are to persevere, because, as was argued in the previous chapter, the workload on pastors appears to be getting heavier.

It is sad but true, pastor, that almost certainly you will not get the thanks and appreciation you deserve for your sacrificial labour from many of the people or organisations you have given your life to serve. But Paul is telling us, in these verses, that you will most definitely be appreciated by your Father in heaven. He will present you with the greatest and most lasting accolade it is possible for anyone to obtain—'a crown of righteousness'.

Bishop Hannington

Such a vision of the crown is the stuff of which Christian heroes are made. It is the raw material from which resilience to the very end is crafted. It brings a motivation to lifelong service permeated with both grit and joy.

The story of James Hannington comes to mind here.[1] So concerned was he for the lost people of East Africa that, in 1882, he left his comfortable vicarage at Hurstpierpoint in Sussex to sail for what was known in those days as 'the dark continent'. The pain of parting from his wife and

---

1. Charles D. Michael, *James Hannington of East Africa* (Pickering & Inglis, 1910).

three children was immense. 'Come back soon, papa!' the family pleaded.

Landing first in Zanzibar, he crossed to the mainland and set out with his porters and helpers for Lake Victoria. But the brutal heat, dangers and deprivations of the journey inland, the diseases and fever he suffered, proved too much. By the summer of the following year he had to return home. 'Forgive me!' he wrote to friends, 'I am a practical failure!'

But he did not give up. With an irresistible concern for Christ's honour and for African people on the road to destruction, he could not stay in England. With a new group of workers and now authorised by the Church of England as Bishop of East Africa, he reached Mombasa (on the coast of modern Kenya) on 24 January 1885. Once again, he set off into the interior with the aim of forging a navigable path to Uganda. Once again, he was overcome on a number of occasions by ferocious bouts of fever. But he pressed on. His desire was ultimately to establish a series of mission stations which would extend from Mombasa up by the Lakes Naivasha and Baringo into Uganda.

The journey was to end in his death. The tribes in Uganda suspected that the white man had come to take their lands. Unwell and weak, Hannington was captured by the native warriors of a capricious tribal king whom he had gone to see, accompanied by just a few helpers. He was held in atrocious conditions before his murder. The details of his last days only came to light as one of his group was later able to purchase his diary from a man involved in killing the bishop.

Eyewitnesses of Hannington's martyrdom later said that, as his assailants closed in around him with their lethal spears, he raised his hand. For a moment they hesitated. Before they killed him, he told them that they were to tell their king that he died for the people of Uganda and that he had purchased the road to their country with his life.

One of his last letters to friends, probably penned by the light of a camp fire, showed how much thoughts of heaven and being received by Jesus sustained him at this time. 'If this is the last chapter of my earthly history,' he wrote, 'then the next will be the first page of the heavenly – no blots and smudges, no incoherence, but sweet converse in the presence of the Lamb.'

And dying with an eye on his eternal reward, he did open the road into Africa. His biographer explains: 'The work received a tremendous impetus by Hannington's martyrdom. Within a few weeks after the news (of his death) came to England, fifty men had offered themselves to the Church Missionary Society for service in the mission field; and Hannington's name has continued ever to be an inspiration to many.'

Here was faith and love that persevered in the task God gave, among the people God loved, all the way to glory. Here was faith that inspired others. Despite setbacks he did not give up. It was resilience right to the end.

We see this same theme in our verses as, from Rome, the apostle Paul, in prison and awaiting execution like James Hannington, finishes his letter.

Paul's departure (4:6-8)

For most of the letter Paul has been exhorting and advising Timothy. The younger man has been in the foreground. But now, as the letter comes to a conclusion Paul begins to talk about himself a little more. The focus switches to Paul as he looks to the future:

> *For I am already being poured out like a drink offering, and the time has come for my departure. I have fought the good fight, I have finished the race, I have kept the faith. Now there is in store for me the crown of righteousness, which the Lord, the righteous Judge, will award to me on that day – and not only to me, but also to all who have longed for his appearing.*

As he comes to the finish of his ministry, Paul looked forward to a crown of righteousness (4:8). What is this crown? It isn't the righteousness of Christ that clothes us, justifies us and fits us for heaven. That's the robe of righteousness. The crown is founded on that righteousness but is different from it. It is an accolade. When we are saved, we are given a righteous status before God. We are forensically wrapped in Christ's righteousness. Legally, we are forever 'right with God' because of what Jesus has done for us. But then we are challenged to become, in practice, what we are in status—righteous people, holy people. So begins the process of sanctification and the path of service. Our salvation never depends on service and sanctification, this second practical righteousness, but our heavenly reward does.

The crown of righteousness is a heavenly reward related to our faithful labours for Christ:

By the grace God has given me, I laid a foundation as an expert builder, and someone else is building on it. But each one should be careful how he builds. For no one can lay any other foundation other than the one already laid, which is Jesus Christ. If any man builds on this foundation using gold, silver, costly stones, wood, hay or straw, his work will be shown for what it is, because the Day will bring it to light. It will be revealed with fire, and the fire will test the quality of each man's work. If what he has built survives, he will receive his reward. If it is burned up, he will suffer loss; he himself will be saved, but only as one escaping through the flames. (1 Cor. 3:10-15)

Blessed are you when people insult you, persecute you and falsely say all kinds of evil against you because of me. Rejoice and be glad, because great is your reward in heaven, for in the same way they persecuted the prophets who were before you. (Matt. 5:11-12)

With such truths as these in mind, Paul encourages Timothy to perseverance (4:8), saying that same reward awaits all who press on in service and long for Christ's appearing. Of course there is a reward for all believers but it is particularly relevant to pastors to whom God has given such a major role in building His church. Recognising our possible future reward is crucial to our resilience. Keeping our eyes on it helps us to see that our labour in the Lord is not in vain (1 Cor. 15:58).

Our psychology

Even secular psychologists realise that a sense of reward and purpose to life is significant. They see that a sense of achievement and that we are heading somewhere is a key factor for resilience.

In her book *Resilience: A Spiritual Project,* Kirsten Birkett cites research concerning the benefits of 'cognitive reappraisal' in making people more resilient. Cognitive reappraisal is 'the ability to monitor and assess negative thoughts and replace them with more positive ones— "finding the silver lining," or finding a meaning in life events.'[2] When we go through tough times but can see that they will result in benefit in the end, we think differently about them. We reframe the situation more positively and that helps us carry on. For the Christian, the great 'silver lining' to the dark clouds of this present fallen world must be heaven and its rewards. Paul reframes his own worst experiences and painful challenges in just this way: 'I consider that our present sufferings are not worth comparing with the glory that will be revealed in us' (Rom. 8:18).

He is being somewhat ironic about his difficulties, but he is even more explicit as he writes to the Corinthians: 'For our light and momentary troubles are achieving for us an eternal glory that far outweighs them all' (2 Cor. 4:17).

Heaven and its rewards enable people to say, 'Yes, it's tough now, but it's worth it!' We could go back and reflect once again on the picture we saw in chapter 2 of the Christian worker as an athlete. How often watching TV coverage of the Olympic games, the post-race interview with the gold medalist turns to the discipline of training? There are early mornings of pounding the roads through the cold, fog and drizzle, or the lonely, lung-bursting

---

2. Kirsten Birkett, *Resilience: A Spiritual Project,* Latimer Studies (Latimer Trust, 2016), page 22.

sessions counting off the lengths at dawn, up and down the swimming pool. But the gold medal makes every moment of it worthwhile.

But we pastors burst our guts for a greater glory, a heavenly glory which is so much more worthwhile.

Our souls

The trouble is, though, we know these things as pastors and we have preached these things, perhaps hundreds of times, often, somehow, we don't feed our souls on them. In the old adage, 'it's in the head but not heart'. We think it, but we don't feel it.

This is frequently the situation with church leaders who should know better. We have lost the art of feeding our souls personally from God's Word. When I first laid down my work as a local church pastor and took up the work of supporting pastors, I spent an afternoon with a man who had been 'pastoring' pastors for a number of years. I learned many helpful lessons as I listened to his wisdom. But here is one very significant thing he pressed upon me. 'If you can do nothing else,' he counselled, 'if you can just get pastors to take their devotions seriously, including prayerfully meditating on the word of God, you will have accomplished a major victory in their lives.' He explained that, under the pressures to be seen to be 'successful', many ministers only read the Bible for sermon preparation. When they open Scripture, they only think about their upcoming engagements to speak, not about their own needs. They are led to focus on the 'seen' parts of their ministry rather than the unseen. And this is to the detriment of their own souls. Forever giving out, they hardly have time to take in.

My mentor that afternoon used a telling illustration. Imagine that the pastor is the cup and the congregation is the saucer. The pastor's work in preaching is to fill the saucer of his hearers with the fresh, life-giving water of the Word. The right way to achieve this is for the 'Pastor Cup' to be so full of biblical, Spirit-empowered truth that it overflows from him into the saucer, into the hearts of the congregation.

'But many,' my friend told me, 'just drill holes through the bottom of the cup. The message goes straight through them and hardly touches the sides.'

Yes, they have studied hard and produced a well-constructed and interesting sermon. But it's never touched their own hearts! They have become professionals in ministry and are no longer awe-struck enthusiasts who can't wait to tell others of the glories of Jesus Christ. Such men struggle to last in ministry.

But Paul is not like that. He feeds on the Word. He lives by faith. He believes what he preaches. Through the written Word of God, existential experience of Christ, the living Word of God, delights him moment by moment. And so the thought of being with Christ and receiving a crown from His hand is all he lives for. And this holds true as his ministry comes to a conclusion. It holds true as even death comes into view. Using those well-known pictures of the soldier and the athlete, which continually colour his mindset, he writes: 'I have fought the good fight, I have finished the race, I have kept the faith.'

The heavenly crown spurs him on to sacrificial living right up to the time of his departure.

Paul's disappointments (4:9-15)

Do your best to come to me quickly, for Demas, because he loved this world, has deserted me and gone to Thessalonica. Crescens has gone to Galatia and Titus to Dalmatia. Only Luke is with me. Get Mark and bring him with you, because he is helpful to me in my ministry. I sent Tychicus to Ephesus. When you come, bring the cloak that I left with Carpus in Troas, and my scrolls, especially the parchments.

Alexander the metalworker did me a great deal of harm. The Lord will repay him for what he has done. You too should be on your guard against him, because he strongly opposed our message.

In these verses, Paul is asking for Timothy to come to him and to bring some items with him. In doing so, he begins to reveal something more of himself—his own needs and vulnerabilities. This resilient apostle is not an iron man. He needs people. He needs things. It reminds us that, though the pastor's primary job is to look after the church, the church does need to look after its pastor.

Paul has been seeking to strengthen fragile Timothy. But now we see that, to some extent, Paul is fragile too. We tend to think of wise, strong Paul ministering to weak and wobbly Timothy. But actually Paul is human as well.

Interestingly, the best people to be pastors and help others are often those who are aware of their own frailties and failures. It is a very difficult truth, which makes the ministry harder, but it is a fact that the best pastors have thin skins. They feel things deeply. That means they are easily hurt. But it also means that they are able to feel for others. They are sensitive leaders who are able to imagine what it's like to be in the other person's shoes. That's how they understand them so well. It means Christ's *golden rule*, 'do to others what you would have them do to you' (Matt. 7:12), can come more easily to them. Their ministry and help has a winsome and gentle appropriateness about it. How many of Christ's sheep have been battered and bruised by the hobnail boots of insensitive church leaders? Often other pastors have to bind up the wounds.

Paul wants Timothy to come. He wants him to bring Mark with him. He wants his cloak. He wants his books and parchments. There are a couple of down-to-earth lessons for pastors which we must not miss here.

Other people can be a source of support, but often they are not

Paul makes these requests in the context of a number of people having left him for various reasons. The departure of others makes him feel his wants. We might be part of an eldership team; we are all part of a congregation. Those others around us help us stand spiritually. Here Paul mentions a number of people who have been part of his missionary team—but it's not encouraging.

- *Paul's apostate*: 'for Demas, because he loved this world, has deserted me and has gone to Thessalonica' (4:10a). This man had shared the work with Paul in past days (Col. 4:14), but now he has abandoned the faith. He has walked out on Paul and the faith. This is a warning to us all in Christian work. Love for Christ and love for the world are mutually exclusive. And sometimes the world appears to win. That must have been shattering for Paul. He thought this man was a Christian, a good brother in Christ. But he turned out to be a fake. What was in Thessalonica that lured Demas? Was it a job, a woman, or just the thought of getting away out of the spiritual battle and its demands?

- *Paul's team*: 'Crescens has gone to Galatia and Titus to Dalmatia. Only Luke is with me' (4:10b, 11a). Once Paul had a sturdy team. Now, besides Paul himself, it's down to just one man! No doubt there were good reasons for Crescens and Titus going. But still it can be lonely and disappointing when the team shrinks. Other situations have had to take priority.

- *Paul's opponent*: 'Alexander the metalworker did me a great deal of harm. The Lord will repay him for what he has done' (4:14). There you are out of love for the lost, seeking to save non-Christians, but some of them turn on you!

- *Paul's deserters*: 'At my first defence, no one came to my support, but everyone deserted me. May it not be held against them' (4:16). Paul had to appear in court in Rome on some charge. It seems some Christians had said something like, 'Yes, we saw what happened, we will be in court to speak up for you, Paul.' But they didn't turn up. They abandoned him probably through fear of the authorities.

There is a lot here to disappoint Paul. Even Christian friends let him down badly. It happens. It happens to pastors. Christians you really thought were your friends turn their backs on you. They show no care. This is tough.

143

But notice Paul is trying hard to maintain a good attitude towards them. It is no good falling into bitterness. It's a real test of our Christianity. 'May it not be held against them' (4:16b). That's hard. That's why perhaps Paul's resilience was greater even than that of James Hannington. The captured bishop faced martyrdom, but at least his Christian brothers had not let him down or abandoned him. On a number of occasions, I have listened to friends in ministry saying something like, 'you expect fiery darts from the world but when it's Christians, it's so hurtful. It makes you wonder if you have just been wasting your time.' But it happens (Pss. 55:12-14; 69:20). It even happened to Christ (Mark 14:37, 50). It is at such points in the ministry that it is particularly important to fix our eyes on Jesus and the heavenly reward. Christians sometimes may not love us, but Christ does. Christians may no longer appreciate us, but Jesus will show His appreciation on the Last Day. But there is another down-to-earth lesson to learn here too.

There is a level of self-care, which is helpful for resilience

God looks after us, but usually He does so by providing means. We are foolish to ignore these if we want to last in ministry. We note here a number of elements in Paul's requests of Timothy. It is plain that Paul is doing what he can to take care of himself.

Paul is trying to do what he can to look after himself *physically*. He wants Timothy to bring that warm cloak before winter (4:21). He is trying to exercise himself *mentally*. We don't know precisely what they are but he wants Timothy to bring the parchments and books, reading materials. He wants to read and study and keep his mind active. Paul is also aware of his needs *socially*. He has lost a number of folk around him. But seeing Timothy would be wonderful. And he wants him to bring Mark. It seems he wants to repair his relationship with Mark who had infuriated Paul by walking out on the first missionary trip in Turkey. That disagreement had led to a parting of ways between Paul and Barnabas. But if his relationship with Mark had not been remade already, now was the time to do it. And, though we may be reading more into the verses than we can actually prove, Mark may have been potentially useful for Paul's ministry because he would bring his Gospel with him based on Peter's eye-witness memories of the life, death and resurrection of Lord Jesus. This would help Paul *spiritually*.

Paul is in a difficult place but he is being sensible. Physically, mentally, socially and spiritually he is trying to use the means God has placed at his disposal to look after himself. We soon lose resilience if we foolishly neglect ourselves or run ourselves into the ground.

Paul's defence (4:16-18)

At my first defence, no one came to my support, but everyone deserted me. May it not be held against them. But the Lord stood at my side and gave me strength, so that through me the message might be fully proclaimed and all the Gentiles might hear it. And I was delivered from the lion's mouth. The Lord will rescue me from every evil attack and will bring me safely to his heavenly kingdom. To him be glory for ever and ever. Amen.

Here we see another immense contrast. Though friends may let you down, the Lord does not. Paul is having to defend himself in court. But really the Lord Himself is his defence counsel.

There might appear to be something of a contradiction between 4:6-8 where Paul speaks of waiting to die, and 4:17, which speaks of being delivered from the lion's mouth (probably not literally, but a colloquialism for acquittal).

If Paul has been delivered, how come he is still expecting to die? Probably what has happened is something like this. At his first court hearing, with the Lord's help, i.e., with Jesus by his side by His Spirit, Paul was acquitted. But now things have deteriorated again somehow. His accusers are determined to do away with him. New charges have been dredged up by his opponents. He has been rearrested. And now, having prevailed in his first defence (the use of the adjective 'first' concerning his defence seems significant) there now has to be a second. There are enemies who are determined to get him executed. But the Lord's help for him at the first hearing has encouraged Paul to know that whatever happens—and it looks like death—'The Lord will rescue me from every evil attack and will bring me safely to his heavenly kingdom. To him be the glory for ever and ever. Amen' (4:18).

Sometimes the Lord delivers us *from* the jaws of death, as with Shadrach, Meshach and Abednego in the fiery furnace. But sometimes he delivers us by taking us *through* the doors of death, as with Stephen, the first Christian martyr:

But Stephen, full of the Holy Spirit, looked up to heaven and saw the glory of God, and Jesus standing at the right hand of God... While they were stoning him, Stephen prayed, 'Lord Jesus, receive my spirit.' Then he fell on his knees and cried out, 'Lord, do not hold this sin against them.' When he had said this, he fell asleep. (Acts 7:55-60)

I am reminded of a dear old saint, Mr Gladwell, who lived at the end of our road and was a member of our church. As he came towards the end of his life I did my best to visit him in hospital. But one day, I went in to the hospital to find that he had passed away. However, a nurse told me, 'It was very strange at the end. It was as if he saw something or someone, sat up in bed, put his arms out and then he was gone!' Sometimes it is by taking us to be with Himself that the Lord delivers us.

Here is the ultimate source of Paul's resilience. At his conversion, he had seen the risen Lord, the conqueror of death, who called him to ministry and that same conqueror of death would take him safely to His heavenly kingdom (4:18). Hence Paul is at peace, unafraid, determined, resilient, preaching Christ to all to the end. The motto of the great missionary to Africa, David Livingstone, concerning his Christian life and work was, 'No reservations, no regrets, no retreat.' That, by God's grace, was Paul's motto too.

Paul's desire (4:19-22)

Greet Priscilla and Aquila and the household of Onesiphorus. Erastus stayed in Corinth, and I left Trophimus sick in Miletus. Do your best to get here before winter. Eubulus greets you, and so do Pudens, Linus, Claudia and all the brothers.

147

The Lord be with your spirit. Grace be with you.

These last few verses are mostly greetings to and from different Christians.

For the church

The list includes a (childless?) married couple, Priscilla and Aquila, who we know from the rest of the New Testament are peripatetic tentmakers, zealous for Christ (Acts 18:1-3; Rom. 16:3-4). Onesiphorus was the head of a household, a family man. Erastus was a high official, the director of public works in the city of Corinth (Rom. 16:23). The fact that he is mentioned on his own may indicate either that he was single or that he was the only one in his family who was a Christian. Then we are told of Trophimus who was not well and had to be left behind—maybe indicating that he had a long-term illness. (Evidently even through the hands of an apostle like Paul, it is not always God's will to heal people.) Then there is a list of folk who have asked Paul to give their greetings to Timothy.

Here is a picture of Christian fellowship between people in different conditions of life. And it is such disparate groups of people who a pastor is called to look after and attend to. The sharing of affectionate greetings speaks of the love and unity of those in Christ, which is surely what Paul and all Christian workers, including Timothy, should desire to promote and enjoy. That is very much part and parcel of the work in which we need to persevere. Though Paul's great charge to Timothy is to 'preach the word' (4:2), we need to remember that preaching is not an end in itself. It is meant to be the means of seeing sinners saved and the church encouraged to loving unity and faithful discipleship in Christ to His glory.

For Timothy

The apostle's final words are for Timothy.

We began this book on resilience by highlighting that the *sine qua non* for pastors and preachers is that they know the Lord personally. This is Paul's great desire for Timothy as he closes his correspondence: 'The Lord be with your spirit'. He wants Timothy not simply to know the facts about Christ but to be experiencing His presence and His enabling in his heart. Paul had known what a difference it had made when he stood in the dock to have that sense in his heart that the Lord was standing at his side (4:17). That is what he desires Timothy to know. It is that which will be a key factor in bringing him through his doubts and fears at this evident time of crisis.

Lastly, Paul writes: 'Grace be with you.' If we try to stand on our deserving or by our own efforts, we will soon fall. Paul reminds Timothy that the gospel is about grace—God's underserved and constant favour in Christ. It is this, not our determination and gritting our teeth which will make us resilient. His last words echo his previous and central great exhortation to Timothy: 'You then, my son, be strong in the grace that is in Christ Jesus.'

Exercise for those in ministry

In this last chapter, Paul has to some extent begun to share his own needs and vulnerabilities. To what extent can you be candid with your own congregation about your own needs? Though you are God's servant, how can you encourage the church not to regard you as some kind of superman but as someone who needs their prayers, while at the same time keeping their respect for you?

Bring this to God in prayer.

Summary

When we get knocked down in ministry, it is easy to conclude that we are not up to the job and it is time to resign. We can think we haven't got what it takes. But the kind of strength required for ministry is not the strength never to waver. We will get floored in ministry. But the secret is to realise that, with God's grace, we can get up again. With God's help, we can, in the words of song-writer Jerome Kern, 'pick ourselves up, dust ourselves off and start all over again'. That's resilience.

To be knocked down does not mean our ministries are over. It doesn't mean we are not good enough. Jesus Himself was laid low—in the grave. But God raised Him from the dead. He stood up again. His ministry continues. And with God as our Father, we too can be 'raised up' to continue our ministry.

The letter of 2 Timothy has an underlying theme of resurrection, which is in Paul's mind as he encourages Timothy to persevere and not give up in Christian work.

- The 'promise ... of life' in 1:1 refers to resurrection.
- For Timothy's gift to be 'fan[ned] into flame' (1:6) carries the same 'come back' idea.
- In 1:10, Paul speaks of Christ having destroyed death and brought immortality.
- There are references in 2 Timothy to the Day of Judgment which imply resurrection (1:18, 4:8).
- Paul tells Timothy to 'remember Jesus Christ, raised from the dead' (2:8).
- He encourages Timothy saying, 'If we died with him, we will also live with him.' (2:11)
- The great error of Hymenaeus and Philetus is their denial of coming resurrection (2:18).
- That God will judge the living and the dead assumes resurrection (4:1).
- Paul's crown awaiting in glory (4:8) implies ultimate resurrection for it will be given on 'that day'.
- When Paul speaks of being brought safely to God's heavenly kingdom, resurrection is in view (4:18).

So it is, that Paul has commended resilience to Timothy. How can we be resilient as pastors and preachers? Pulling together the practical points we have seen, we can describe a resilient pastor with the following headlines. A resilient pastor is:

- Called to the work
- Crucified to self
- Confident in God's grace
- Clear as to his priorities
- Conscious of his limitations

- Cared for by companions
- Candid with a praying church

May the Lord make us resilient in His glorious service.

Also available from Christian Focus Publications …

CALLED?

PASTORAL GUIDANCE
FOR THE DIVINE CALL
TO GOSPEL MINISTRY

MICHAEL A. MILTON

978-1-5271-0112-8

Called?

Pastoral Guidance for the Divine Call to Gospel Ministry

MICHAEL A. MILTON

Only those who have an undeniable calling from God will be fit for the challenges and strains of the ministry life. But how do you test a calling and how do you proceed if you are certain its legitimacy?

From the theology of being called, to selecting a seminary, to beginning life as a pastor, Michael Milton looks to the Word of God for answers and guidance, as well as drawing on his own experience as a Presbyterian minister.

When asked for advice as to how to discern a call to ministry, I will now say with confidence, 'You should read Mike Milton's book. It will answer most if not all of your questions.'

Derek Thomas
Senior Minister of Preaching and Teaching, First Presbyterian Church, Columbia, South Carolina

The Scripture–soaked wisdom offered here will help put godly pastors in the pulpits.

Michael J. Kruger
President and Professor of New Testament, Reformed Theological Seminary, Charlotte, North Carolina

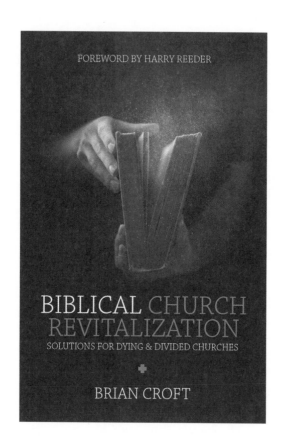

FOREWORD BY HARRY REEDER

BIBLICAL CHURCH
REVITALIZATION
SOLUTIONS FOR DYING & DIVIDED CHURCHES

✚

BRIAN CROFT

978-1-7819-1766-4

Biblical Church Revitalization

Solutions for Dying & Divided Churches

BRIAN CROFT

There is a unique and special power and testimony in not just a vibrant local church full of life, but an old historic one that had lost its way, that was on life support, and into which God saw fit to breathe life once again. Biblical Church Revitalization calls us to an intentional commitment to church revitalization in the face of dying and divided churches.

Some books are written from ivory towers. Biblical Church Revitalization is not one of them. Brian Croft writes about church revitalization as one who has labored in the trenches of this work for several years ... this book is a "must read" on the topic of revitalizing churches.

TIMOTHY K. BEOUGHER
Billy Graham Professor of Evangelism, The Southern Baptist Theological Seminary, Louisville, Kentucky

I loved this book. Immensely practical and completely realistic. This should be a must read for all pastors and church planters when it comes to handling expectations of the ministry. Very, very good. Get on it.

MEZ MCCONNELL
Pastor, Niddrie Community Church and Ministry Director of 20Schemes

Christian Focus Publications

Our mission statement –

STAYING FAITHFUL

In dependence upon God we seek to impact the world through literature faithful to His infallible Word, the Bible. Our aim is to ensure that the Lord Jesus Christ is presented as the only hope to obtain forgiveness of sin, live a useful life and look forward to heaven with Him.

Our books are published in four imprints:

CHRISTIAN
FOCUS

Popular works including biographies, commentaries, basic doctrine and Christian living.

CHRISTIAN
HERITAGE

Books representing some of the best material from the rich heritage of the church.

MENTOR

Books written at a level suitable for Bible College and seminary students, pastors, and other serious readers. The imprint includes commentaries, doctrinal studies, examination of current issues and church history.

CF4•K

Children's books for quality Bible teaching and for all age groups: Sunday school curriculum, puzzle and activity books; personal and family devotional titles, biographies and inspirational stories – because you are never too young to know Jesus!

Christian Focus Publications Ltd,
Geanies House, Fearn, Ross-shire,
IV20 1TW, Scotland, United Kingdom.
www.christianfocus.com
blog.christianfocus.com